Do it while you still can:

motorcycle escapades and tribulations

Nick Adams

Copyright © 2021 Nicholas R. Adams

All rights reserved.

ISBN: 9798462859816
Imprint: Independently published

Contents

INTRODUCTION 1

LOOKING BACK 2

TWO STEPS FORWARDS, THREE STEPS BACK 17

AUTOMATICALLY RIDING 32

   1986 SUZUKI CAVALCADE LXE 46

DO IT WHILE YOU STILL CAN! 55

FIGHTING WITH MY PANTHER 88

MISSISSAGI 119

THE PANTHER RIDES AGAIN 135

THE FRANKENBEAST 143

ONE MAN'S MEAT 152

SOME RANDOM THOUGHTS 156

ON GETTING OFF YOUR BACKSIDE 167

ACKNOWLEDGMENTS

A big thank you, whoever you are, for buying this little book. The tiny income I get from book sales goes towards more fuel, more trips, spare parts, and the occasional beer, so cheers.

If this is your first dip into these murky waters, many thanks for taking a chance. And if you've read my stuff before, I'm especially pleased that you've considered it entertaining enough to give this one a whirl.

My family (Chris, Sam, Emily, and Alex) must put up with me monopolizing the garage, being away from time to time, and being unresponsive when I return. They are patient when hearing the same stories over and over, as I try and turn a few memories and a few photographs into words. Thank you all.

INTRODUCTION

If you're looking for epic travel stories to exotic places, tales of bribery at borders, or of being lost and penniless in foreign lands you've come to the wrong place. There are many fine books about lengthy motorcycle journeys, full of excitement and derring-do, but this isn't one of them.

Within these pages you'll find some short motorcycle travel stories, some moaning and groaning about various mechanical problems and their eventual fixes, a couple of short road tests, and a fair bit of griping about the things I like and dislike about motorcycling. It's a grab-bag of bits and pieces I've written over the last year or so.

Some of the chapters are articles I've written for 'RealClassic' magazine that I've expanded or adapted for this environment, so I apologize to RC subscribers if parts seem strangely familiar.

Mostly though, it's about riding older bikes, having fun riding and, most importantly, of seizing the day. Life is short – live it to the full.

LOOKING BACK

When I look back down the dark, narrow, and increasingly foggy tunnel of my memory I can see that my history of motorcycle repair is a sad tale of incompetence, frustration, skinned knuckles, and unnecessary expenditure. In one of my other books, I briefly mentioned my BSA Royal Star, talking glowingly about how it had been a trusty companion and reliable commuter during my regular journeys from Norfolk to my mum's place south of Birmingham. All that was true. It really was a fine bike that didn't give me a moment's trouble until…

I'd met a girl on an archaeological dig in Dorchester and, as our relationship progressed, we decided to take a tour of Scotland on the BSA. All should have been well, except that as I was returning on the bike to Norfolk I noticed a disturbing chirping coming from deep inside the engine at anything above an idle, especially when the engine wasn't under load. In the days before the internet, we didn't have instant access to millions of experts and countless videos demonstrating sundry problems, so I had to rely on my Haynes workshop manual and the wisdom of the few people I knew who knew anything about motorbikes to diagnose the problem.

Ultimately, it became clear that the most likely culprit was the main bearings, and the only way to be sure was to tear into the engine. At the time, I was living with friends in a rural farmhouse in Norfolk, so I did what any sensible young lad would do – I removed the engine from the bike, carried it into the house, and took it to pieces on the living room carpet. I'm assuming I must have made some attempt to keep oil from drooling everywhere, but if I did, I can't remember. Anyway, our carpet was a living thing of spilled beer, crushed crisps, and cigarette ash, so a little engine oil wasn't going to bother anyone much.

I was highly motivated to get the bike running again so abandoning my usual strategy of boldly going where I'd never been before, I religiously followed the 'tear down' instructions in the manual, found a source for replacement bearings, then carefully reassembled the engine using the manuals exceptionally helpful 'reassembly is the reverse of disassembly' as my guide.

And 'Blast Me', as Norfolk primitives have been known to say, the darn thing ran afterwards. I was frankly astonished and thrilled.

Within a matter of days, we were loaded up and heading to Scotland. We cruised up the west coast, crossed on the ferry from Kyle of Lochalsh to Skye, rode past Torridon, Ullapool, Scourie - which sounds like a distressing abdominal complaint - and Durness, before riding the delightful north coast road across to Thurso and the ferry to Orkney. On Orkney we tripped around exploring standing stones and chambered tombs, loving the treeless, windswept islands and wild coastal scenery before it was time to head south once more.

The bike always started, used an acceptably small amount of fuel, was surprisingly comfortable considering we had all kinds of camping and personal gear strapped to it, managed the hills without complaint or distress, and returned us home at the end of a couple of weeks without the slightest hiccup. After years of irritating, and to me, completely baffling problems with lesser bikes and scooters, I'd finally managed to achieve a motorcycle fix that actually worked. For a while.

In the months after, the main bearing chirping gradually reappeared. Apparently, I should have paid closer attention to the part where the manual was talking about 'shimming for end float' - whatever that was supposed to mean - but I managed to sell the bike before it self-destructed, so for once, all ended well – at least for me.

The BSA was the last in a whole series of bikes I owned before I headed to Canada and lost track of motorcycling for almost thirty years. But there were others. Memory is a peculiar thing – at least mine is. Some of the fragments that remain are crystal clear. I can see and feel the moment – it's as if the whole experience is still there even if the context and the broader picture has been lost. Let me explain.

I have this strong mental image of riding through Birmingham in the early morning grey-zone, edging gradually west towards Wales. I can no longer remember specifically where I was headed, or why. It was probably to meet up with friends for one of the many hiking / camping trips we used to take - but I remember the ride there and I remember the bike.

I was riding on damp roads through one of Birmingham's more affluent suburbs. It must have been early Saturday morning. There was almost no traffic, and few people were moving. The Ariel Leader 250 I had recently bought was loaded with camping gear, its metal panniers full of clothes and tent, with my sleeping bag, undoubtedly wrapped in plastic, strapped on the rack behind. The two-stroke twin motor was burbling along quietly, its exhaust muted through two large chrome silencers. Suddenly, I had to brake at a pedestrian crossing.

I can no longer see for whom or why, but that moment is forever fossilized in my mind. I can smell the wet road and the faint odor of two-stroke oil, I can see the Belisha beacon flashing next to the black and white striped crossing. I can hear the muted and surprisingly reliable tick-over of the Ariel as I waited for whomever had caused me to stop to cross in front of me. And I can feel the air moving past my helmet as I accelerated away.

Unlike most of the small motorcycles and scooters I'd owned, the Ariel Leader was proving to be a revelation. It started instantly any time I wanted to go somewhere. It ran smoothly and quietly. It was comfortable to ride no matter how long the journey. It handled and braked responsively. It was relatively cheap to run, giving good fuel mileage. The weather protection behind the enormous wind and leg shields was excellent. It was even surprisingly fast, having no trouble cruising at sixty miles an hour. So why wasn't I enraptured?

The Ariel transported me to my rendezvous in Wales and home again without any issues, breakdowns, or troubles. How do I know if I can't even remember where I went? Well, when you're stuck by the side of the road with a bike that won't start, has blown its engine, the electrics have fried, the carburetor is gummed up or you've run out of fuel, you tend to remember. That grim, sinking feeling in the pit of your stomach tends to fix those memories, especially when, in the days before roadside recovery, it almost always meant the ignominy and ball-shriveling necessity of calling your dad. My Dad never let me down. He always turned up to rescue me, eventually, even if I had had to wait for hours. And it was always worse if he took a quick look at whichever bike or scooter I was on and tightened a nut or cleaned a spark plug and the darn thing started again.

But none of this happened with the Ariel. It was resolutely reliable. So why did I sell it, only to be replaced by something uncomfortable and untrustworthy? Why didn't I keep it and ride many thousands of happy miles on it? I suppose the short answer is, I was a daft teenager: always on the lookout for the next exciting experience and woefully subject to the opinions of others.

The Ariel was a practical motorcycle. Its extensive metal bodywork wasn't sexy. Its performance was dependable not exciting. It had no panache. It was the kind of motorcycle that your grandpa might contentedly ride each day to his job on the production line at Dagenham or Cowley. It was not the bike a hot-blooded teenager wanted to be seen riding. To use modern terminology, it just wasn't cool.

That Ariel was one of the best bikes I ever had. But now I think about it, I realise it was the nineteen-sixties equivalent of the Honda Pacific Coast – the bike I had wanted so much to like but didn't (but more on this later). In creating a practical motorcycle which did everything well, both Honda and Ariel had produced machines totally devoid of any sparkle. And without the sparkle, you might just as well avoid the rain, cold and discomfort and drive a car.

Thinking about the Ariel has reminded me of some of the bikes I've regretted selling. It's a small number, because usually by the time I'm ready to sell a bike, I've found myself less interested in it than I previously was, it has some characteristic that irks me, or I find I'm just not riding it enough to justify hanging on to it.

First and foremost of my regrets, and the bike I'd most like to have back, is the 1950 Panther M100 I had when I was a stupid youth. I had bought the bike from a girlfriend's brother for a ridiculously small amount of money. The bike was in perfect original condition. Being fashion conscious teenagers, affected by the chopper craze of the time, my friend John and I hacked and abused that bike until it loosely conformed to that weird and impractical style, in the process losing much of its original usefulness and dignity.

My regret has nothing to do with monetary value. Although the cost of well-preserved Panthers has risen over the last few years, they still occupy one of the lower tiers of vintage bike desirability. Lacking the flair of sporting classic like the Velocette Venom, the BSA Gold Star or, further back in time, anything from the Rudge company, Panthers are seen as worthy, but pedestrian 'Grey Porridge' and their resale figures reflect that. But even if Panthers changed hands for Brough numbers, it wouldn't make any difference to me. My Panther was a good, honest, fully functional, and rather lovely, character-full motorcycle which I foolishly abused and sacrificed on the altar of transitory fashion.

I know motorcycles are just machines of metal, rubber, leather, glass, and plastic; that they have no feelings; that they're just inert lumps until provided with a form of life through spark, fuel, and human desire for movement, but if that bike could have spoken, I'm sure it would have cursed me in the strongest Yorkshire accent.

If, by some magic I could roll back the clock and extract that bike from my own hands I would. I would treat it well, ride it often and cherish its old-fashioned appearance and performance. Sadly, saving my pennies and buying a different 1950 Panther M100 wouldn't cut it. It's THAT bike I want back, not one like it. And that will never happen. I suspect it was broken up as scrap long ago. It's a sadness and burden I will continue to carry.

In recent years quite a few bikes have passed through my hands. Each has done service for a while then been moved on to greener pastures. Even though there was nothing wrong with it, the Suzuki GT750 two-stroke triple I bought for pocket change, got running and tarted up a bit, didn't really appeal to me and was soon gone. It was one of the very few bikes I made a profit on, selling it for almost double what I paid.

My dalliance with big modern cruisers lasted a couple of years. My Yamaha Royal Star Tour Deluxe was beautifully made, powerful and surprisingly agile, but despite loving the delicious V4 engine, I never quite managed to find a seating position that worked for me. I am accustomed to sitting on a bike as if it's a horse: back straight or a slight forward lean, feet below the hips, arms loose on the bars.

2007 Yamaha Royal Star Tour Deluxe

Cruisers encourage you to slump, placing far too much pressure on the sitting bones. I know some people swear by the 'feet forwards' riding position and can ride long distances in comfort. However, after putting up with never feeling entirely comfortable, both with the seat and the style for about 20,000 miles, I traded it for a 2007 Moto Guzzi Breva 1100.

You might think that a modern Moto Guzzi would have scratched all my motorcycling itches. The riding position was comfortable, the seat was superb, the engine was vastly faster and more powerful than any of my other Guzzis, and yet I never really bonded with it. I covered many miles on the Breva, but since I sold it, I've barely given it a second thought.

But I do think about my 1974 Moto Guzzi Nuovo Falcone. Slow, clunky, softly sprung, unusual and almost preternaturally invisible to other motorcyclists, the Nuovo Falcone oozed character, but apparently only to me. Other riders saw a small, odd motorbike, barely interesting enough to warrant a wave or a companionable nod in passing. Parked amid other bikes it seemed to disappear, its muted grey-green military paint acting as camouflage.

The performance of the Nuovo Falcone has been the subject of much mirth and derision. Lethargic, sluggish, languid, slothful, and listless could be used to describe the NF's less than sprightly acceleration. It doesn't so much accelerate as gather speed; the unimpressive forward momentum further impeded by the laggardly performance of the gearbox which simply won't be hurried. And when you've finally made it to top gear, it's a struggle to edge past 60 miles an hour and your speed drops dramatically if you encounter a hill or a headwind.

Is this starting to sound truly awful? For those who equate motorcycles with speed, the NF would seem like a nightmare, but here's the thing – it's lovely, charming, engaging and fun to ride, as long as you have the right mind-set. I rode my Nuovo Falcone all over northern Ontario and northern Quebec on multiple tours, often racking up six-hundred-mile days. Once it was rolling it was happy to roll all day. The soft springs and sprung seat were superbly comfortable. It always started, stayed oil tight, and was supremely reliable. The gearbox was a bit tricky, often ending up in third at intersections when I thought I was aiming for first, but you learn to live we these things and it never really bothered me.

"So, if you loved this bike so much, why did you sell it?" I hear you ask. Well, one of areas in which the NF surprised me was its relative lack of torque at low revs. I'd grown up riding the Panthers which are famous for their 'grunt' and was shocked to find the NF needed a few revs to really get moving. It was more like riding a modern Kawasaki KLR than an old British single. When the chance finally arrived for me to get my hands on another Panther (see below) I jumped at it. Two big singles in the garage seemed one too many, so the Nuovo Falcone was sold to pay for the Panther.

In an ideal world I'd have both, but there are limits to what one's garage space, personal finances and wife's tolerance can abide, so the NF had to go. But I do miss it.

My other regret – and this is rather a minor one as I never really got the chance to explore the bikes properly – is that I never did get to grips with the two Yamaha Venture Royale 1300's that I'd bought for next-to-nothing with the intention of making one big touring bike out of two. These bikes have the reputation of being Honda Gold Wing's faster and sportier competitor. Built around an unburstable V4 engine – detuned from the mighty V-Max - and sporting full bodywork including windscreen, panniers and top box, these road couches were designed for cross-continental touring. I remember my excitement of going to view the first one. As I drove along, trailer in tow, I was singing:

"Head out on the Highway, Looking for a Venture…". Pathetic, I know.

My Ventures were fairly rough. Both had excellent engines (once I'd cleaned the carbs) but one would slip out of second gear while the other had cracked and damaged body work. The second gear issue is a well-known problem on the bikes built before 1985. Apparently, a split washer in the gearbox wasn't made of sufficiently hardened steel and eventually wears, allowing the gear to slip. The cost of the replacement washer is a trifle, but the repair requires a full engine-out tear down, so inevitably it rarely got done. Some people continued to ride their bikes by skipping over second gear, while others either just parked them or sold them to unsuspecting buyers.

I intended to strip the good bodywork from the bike with the gear issue and plaster it on to the good bike with the broken panels. But I never did. I was halfway through tearing the bikes apart and had multiple boxes of parts littering my garage floor and two partly disassembled bike carcasses under tarps in my driveway, when my heart troubles started to take over my life. With bypass surgery and a long period of recovery looming, I asked my ever-generous and helpful friend Norm to see if he could sell them for me. By the time I was out of the hospital and back at home both Ventures had disappeared.

I had only ever ridden the bike with the slipping second gear a couple of miles but had found the power of the Yamaha V4 seductive and the riding experience surprisingly enjoyable. I'd had visions of pleasant days out on country roads, and longer tours to distant places with my wife

Chris, but it wasn't to be – at least on the Venture.

I still find myself looking lustfully whenever a Venture surfaces on the local on-line advertisements, but these days I have the mighty Suzuki Cavalcade – also a V4 – to scratch that particular itch.

Although I've made way through quite a few bikes over the years, I just don't get why some people swap bikes like their underwear, constantly changing, constantly searching for something new. I suppose they are addicted to that thrill that comes with exploring the characteristics and capabilities of a new machine. As soon as that first excitement has worn off, then it's on to the next one. I've heard people say things like 'life is short and there are so many bikes to experience', and it's true – there is a host of desirable bikes out there, just waiting to be explored – but do these folks ever really experience any of the bikes that flow through their hands like water? I'm not sure they do.

I'm closer to the other end of the spectrum. Once I have owned and ridden a bike, I tend to hang on to it and have the hardest time letting it go – even bikes I wasn't particularly keen on, or which seemed surplus to my requirements.

My 1972 Moto Guzzi Eldorado is here to stay though. Battle scarred and tatty, it nevertheless manages to give me pleasure whenever I ride it. Over the years we've settled into each other. No other bike I ride or have ridden feels so much a part of me. I find myself choosing it for long distance, multi-day rides when other more suitable, probably more reliable bikes in my garage would make more sense. For me, it has a magic that other bikes just don't have. It has worked its way under my skin.

Now, before you start cruising the internet for your own old Guzzi, a word of warning. This is a personal thing, and I'm certainly not trying to encourage anyone to rush out and buy the first old Guzzi 'Loop' they come across. You would probably find the stone-age suspension, languid performance, marginal brakes and ponderous – if stable – handling the precise opposite of what you find endearing in a motorcycle. If I had any sense at all, I would too. Bikes of this vintage require a hands-on approach to ownership. Ignition points get dirty. Carburetor jets get blocked. With no filtration, oil must be changed regularly. Maintenance is constant, and it would be foolish to head off on a long journey without a comprehensive tool kit and the knowledge of how to use it. Unscheduled roadside stops are expected, yet it's rarely anything that can't be fixed with a little fiddling.

1972 Moto Guzzi Eldorado

I'm embarrassed to say that, because of my writing and Youtube videos, I've been partially responsible for influencing otherwise sensible people to do exactly that. For some, it has been a happy experience. For others, the bikes simply didn't live up to their expectations and, for them at least, didn't reveal any magic – or anything special at all. So, beware. My affection for my Eldorado is an entirely personal thing. Others would almost certainly find it boring, tatty, unreliable, and tedious.

Unreliable? Well, yes and no. In many of my road-trip stories I've talked about having to stop to do little fixes and workarounds because some little thing had either stopped working or was impeding performance. It would be naive to assume you can head across the country on a fifty-year-old motorcycle and not have something that needs adjusting or goes wrong. And as you'll see in one of the chapters which follow, parts can, and do eventually fail.

As motorcycles (and other vehicles) have become more reliable, so have they become much more complex. The handbook for my 1960 Panther M120 provides detailed instructions on how to decoke the engine, check and adjust the valves, set valve and ignition timing, and perform a host of other normal maintenance tasks. It was assumed the owner would have the skill and understanding to do these things – or, at least, could follow well-written instructions to get them done. This is not a workshop manual mind, only to be used by factory-trained technicians with all the special tools and a surgically clean workshop. This is the owners guide, and these tasks were expected to be done by the owner in their garden shed or on the street, with only the most basic tools. These days, even changing the oil is beyond the capabilities of many motorcyclists and would probably void their warranty if they tried.

My most modern motorcycle, the 1986 Suzuki Cavalcade, which you will also meet in the following pages, has its own share of quirks and peculiarities, but so far at least, has proven to be wonderfully reliable. It's a huge lug of a thing – probably far more motorcycle than I, or anyone else for that matter, really needs – yet it displays its relative modernity in the smoothness with which it runs and the precision (for a gigantic beast) with which it handles and brakes.

The upside of modern motorcycles is that they have become vastly more reliable than their predecessors. Nowadays, you push a button, the machine roars to life and you head off for the horizon, the computer perfectly matching the fuel and sparks for instant smooth running and performance. There's no longer any need for arcane starting tricks involving tickling carbs, finding top-dead-centre, and endangering body parts by lurching on a kick-start. And yet, I can't help feeling that some of the joy of motorcycle ownership has been lost along the way.

TWO STEPS FORWARDS, THREE STEPS BACK[1]

This is a cautionary tale of how one should be careful not to allow one's reach to exceed one's grasp.

How is it that you can park a bike for the winter, go to ride it in the spring, and it has developed a mysterious fault while sitting idly in the garage? When I parked my beloved Moto Guzzi Eldorado at the end of 2017 it was running well. If it seemed a little hesitant to engage first gear occasionally, I put it down to the foibles of respectable old age and hard use. We were closing in on 100,000 miles, 65,000 of which I had personally added since I bought it in 2008. I had no reason to think that I was about to encounter a major issue.

Despite the deep snow in the Ontario bush and the sub-zero temperatures, January 26th, 2018, brought clear roads – clear enough at least for a quick sixty-mile loop to remind me that, after a couple of months of being housebound by the weather, I could still ride. I hauled the Eldorado out of the garage, fired it up and headed north. At first all seemed fine, but whenever I slowed, I could hear a disturbing whirring that wasn't there the previous

---

[1] *An abbreviated version of this was included as part of the preamble to my 'Eldorado to the Klondike' story. Here's the full, grim tale, as originally published in 'RealClassic' magazine No's 183/185)*

November. Naively I assumed it was clutch trouble, so I pulled the bike to pieces to see if I could detect the problem.

1972 Moto Guzzi Eldorado

Because the V-twin Moto Guzzis have a longitudinal crankshaft and a dry clutch, to get at it you have to remove the panniers and toolboxes, the rear wheel, the swinging arm and drive shaft, the battery and battery tray, then lift the mudguard and wiring out of the way, basically working your way forwards removing everything behind the gearbox. It sounds complicated but once you've done it a few times it's very straightforward and relatively painless. The starter motor is fixed to the gearbox housing by two bolts. Once it is removed, you can unbolt the gearbox from the bellhousing and wiggle it out of the frame, being careful not to crush your fingers between the heavy box and the frame parts.

I soon had the gearbox sitting on the garage floor and the clutch exposed. Thinking that perhaps a clutch spring had broken, I unbolted the clutch and inspected all its parts. No, everything seemed fine, so I bolted it back together. Next, I wondered whether the clutch-thrust bearing was worn out. This little needle roller bearing fits within a tunnel through the gearbox case, part way along the clutch rod. It's a delicate little thing with tiny rollers. I was confident that it was the cause of the mystery noise, so I sent money off to MgCycle in Wisconsin and waited.

With astonishing speed, the parts arrived. Once I'd recovered from the cost of the shipping, the exchange rate, the import duty, and the provincial taxes which almost doubled the price, I headed back out to the garage to install the new bearing. Gearbox, starter, battery tray, and all the other parts were bolted back in place, and once again the bike was wheeled into the sunlight. I turned on the fuel, turned the key, the engine started...and annoyingly, so did the noise. Oh blast!

Clearly wishful thinking had got the better of me. Once again, I attacked the Eldo, stripping parts with giddy speed, tossing all the bolts and small bits into a tray. I no longer needed to lay stuff out carefully as by now I knew exactly which bits went where.

Now that I was sure the problem lay within the gearbox itself, I dithered about what to do next. Helpful comments from other Guzzi fanatics suggested that since the box was simple and robust, it should be well within my capabilities to strip it, replace the worn-out or malfunctioning parts, and bolt it back together again. I was less confident, but with the assurances of my colleagues, and with the aid of two very detailed gearbox strip guides I downloaded from the internet, I set to work.

I was rather surprised at how easily it all came apart, and in truth, it didn't seem all that complicated: four shafts, a few cogs, selector forks and a few meaty bearings stuck firmly in the cases. As I removed it, the shifter return spring fell apart in my hands, so for that reason alone, I was glad I'd braved the mysteries inside the box. I stuck a finger in each of the bearings and gave them a whirl. Most seemed to turn smoothly, but one was decidedly a little on the sticky side. Once again, I sent off an order to MgCycle who were able to supply most of the bearings. I was able to acquire one of the more obscure bearings from a source in Germany.

My new-found courage didn't extend to removing the bearings myself: I left that, and the installation of their replacements, to my local machine shop. It didn't take them long and I was soon filling the case with shafts and cogs again, doing my best to strictly adhere to the instructions. Everything seemed to click into place properly, and since I didn't have any left-over bits, I bolted the case back together, filled it with the correct amount of 80/90 gear oil, and started the tedious business of reassembling the back half of the bike.

By now it was the beginning of November, the Eldorado had been off the road since spring, and early winter snow and freezing temperatures were rapidly approaching. I was extremely thankful that I'd had other bikes to ride so the riding year hadn't been a complete disaster. Ever the optimist, I was hoping to get one decently long ride on the Eldorado in before the snow came.

It didn't happen. I started the bike, engaged first gear and rode out onto the road. As I accelerated and changed through second into third, it started making some horrible, grinding, screeching noises. I quickly turned around and gingerly headed home. I was almost at my driveway and doing no more than 10mph when the gearbox locked up solid, my rear tire laying a nice back stripe down the asphalt. Oh blast – or words to that effect!

I was done with mucking about. After checking around with a few people, I located a long-time Guzzi mechanic in the Eastern Townships of Quebec, arranged to deliver the gearbox for a complete overhaul, and once again extracted it from the bike. I was hoping to be able to ride the 160 miles to the workshop as I had discovered that the whole gearbox fit neatly under the seat of my Suzuki Burgman scooter. I always prefer to ride if I can and it seemed a suitably bizarre thing to do, but cold weather and poor road conditions had finally arrived. I chickened out and took the truck.

I soon heard back from the mechanic. He had stripped the box, finding a mess of chipped and shattered gears, a bent output (lay) shaft and a cracked case. It was fixable, but he advised me that the best plan was to locate a used replacement gearbox then build up one good one from the best parts of two. After a week or two of looking he found one on eBay for a price that didn't make my eyes bleed. Fortunately, it turned out to be in remarkably good condition. It was from a slightly later generation of Guzzis. Only the speedometer drive take-up was in a different location. By switching its end-case with the one from my gearbox, it became a perfect replacement for my sorry mess of metal filings.

A full year had now passed since I first noticed that disturbing whirring. My Eldorado was all back together and had a functioning gearbox. The shift pattern is reversed from the original one up, four down, but that doesn't matter, I'm used to different gearbox change patterns on my bikes. I had the bike running and the gears engaged smoothly and quietly, but sadly new issues arose.

I don't know whether I just wasn't noticing the noises before, whether I was in a state of denial, or that somehow gremlins crept into my bike during its year-long lay-up, but during my first 'check the new gearbox' ride I couldn't overlook the disturbing clunking emanating from deep in the bowels of the engine once the oil was warm. Under light load it sounded fine, but during acceleration a dull hammering would appear. Ever optimistic, I decided the ignition must be too far advanced, so I adjusted the timing perfectly to specs. No change. I retarded it slightly. No change. The dull knocking persisted. After racking my brain for something to explain the new noise, I sadly had to conclude that when the gearbox locked up solid, the chain reaction of all that rotating metal mass coming to an instant, screeching halt damaged something. Sadly, it looked as though it was time for another tear down and an engine rebuild before the Eldorado could return to the road.

I don't regret the many false starts and mistakes I made along the way, but if there's silver lining, these disasters have reconfirmed what I knew all along: I'm no mechanic. I can do basic stuff – points, carbs, valve clearances and gasket replacements – but when it comes to serious mechanical work where skill, knowledge and precision are required, it's best (for me) to bite the metaphorical bullet and put the work into the hands of someone who knows what they are doing.

Once I'd recovered from the shock of this sad discovery, I extracted the Eldorado's engine from the frame and found a willing guru to do the work. I was determined to pass the Eldorado's 100,000-mile landmark eventually although it looked as though it wouldn't be as soon as I'd hoped. But until that time came, I had other bikes to ride and places to go. But whichever bike I chose, a big part of me was always thinking, 'I wish I was riding the Eldorado'.

Well, I found a willing guru. Yves Foucher of Montecristo-moto in Quebec, who had just provided me with the replacement gearbox, was quite happy to take on the task of rebuilding the Eldorado's engine for me as well.

Always looking for short-cuts, I decided to see whether it was possible to extract the engine from the frame but leave the gearbox in place. Just then, I couldn't face having the tear the whole rear end of the bike apart as well. I had already taken the heads and cylinders off, finding that one of the pistons was in a sorry state, looking scorched and scratched. By moving the swinging arm back, I was able to create just enough free space to wiggle the engine off the gearbox studs then tip it sideways out of the frame. It's a good job I'm not too fussy about aesthetics as I managed to gouge some nasty grooves in the paintwork – but nothing that couldn't be fixed with a brush and a bit of black paint. I boxed everything up in three neatly labelled containers and headed east again.

Heading to Yves

Regardless of what other messes Yves found, I had already decided to replace the cylinders and pistons with new, high-tech Nikisil Gilardonis sourced from Scramblercycle in Cameron, Wisconsin. I'd dealt with the owner Kevin Hahn before when ordering an alternator kit and found him responsive and reliable. That his prices were also the best was a bonus. My Eldorado had been running with 949cc cylinders and pistons for the last 65,000 miles but I opted to go back to the standard 844cc with new 83mm bores. From everything I'd read and experienced, the larger cylinders provide marginally more torque at the expense of a bit of smoothness.

Yves kept me up to date with progress as he disassembled and investigated my engine. I was particularly happy to get this report:

- Crank journals - excellent no scratches or visible wear and they measure perfect.
- Big end connecting rods inserts - excellent no scratches or visible wear and they measure perfect.
- Crankshaft / crankcase end supports front and rear - excellent condition no scratches or visible wear and they measure perfect.
- Timing gears, excellent condition no scratches or visible wear and they measure perfect.
- Camshaft, good some shallow scratches that could be polished off.
- Cam followers, all have cam surface scores/pitted and should be replaced or refaced.
- Oil pump - is not perfect with wear on the outer part of the gears and pump inner body. It is probably still pumping a steady flow but not optimum for a plain bearing crankshaft and should be replaced with a new unit if available.
- Connecting-rods - look good but will be checked for straightness and cracks and also weighed.
- Fly-wheel - very good.

I added an oil pump to my Scramblercycle order and got Kevin to send the whole lot directly to Yves.

A couple of weeks after he got the parts I got the word from Yves that my engine was finished and ready to collect. Once again, I hit the highway. 186 miles each way may seem a long way to go for an engine rebuild but Canada is a big country and skilled Guzzi specialists are thin on the ground.

Before long I was back in the garage heaving the heavy lump into the frame. It all went surprisingly well. Once it was all bolted together, I tried to start the engine. It coughed, spluttered, and wouldn't start, seemingly eager to use the carbs as an exhaust system. I checked the timing. Like an idiot, I'd set the distributor 180 degrees off.

OK. Time for a ride. I wheeled the Eldorado into the sunlight and headed down the road. It was bucking and burping – things I knew which could be fixed with a little carb cleaning and tweaking – but took off like a scorched cat. Plenty of power, oodles of torque, and a happy rider, until the clutch lever suddenly came loose, and my hand and the bike shuddered to a halt. Thinking I'd not adjusted the cable properly first time around, I took up the slack with the adjusters and started off. A few yards later it happened again. My next thought was that the adjuster screw on the clutch lever at the back of the gearbox had stripped its threads – but no, all seemed normal there. I fussed, fumed, and fiddled until well after dark.

As I lay in bed my monkey-brain was hyper-active, working through my mental diagram of the Eldo's innards, finally concluding that the only answer was to pull the gearbox again. Sleep obviously wasn't going to happen anytime soon, so at 1AM, doing my best not to wake Chris, I got up, pulled on my garage clothes, and headed downstairs.

Off came the toolboxes, the battery, the seat, the fuel tank, and the rear wheel. Once again wires were disconnected, linkages removed and sundry bits and pieces either taken off or pushed out of the way. By now I was an expert in tearing the bike apart. Loose bits were just thrown in a heap. I knew exactly which nuts and bolts went where, and which tools were required at each stage. I was flying.

By 2AM I had the gearbox out of the frame and on the floor. A few minutes later the clutch was apart, double checked, and reassembled. I pulled the clutch pushrod and thrust bearing from its tunnel through the gearbox. Hmm.

Something's not right here. Some clown (that would be me) had incorrectly installed the thrust bearing. I carefully laid out all the pieces, examined them for damage or flaws, double checked the diagram in my Guzzi parts book and reassembled.

Sticking the gearbox back in the bike was so easy now I could have done it in my sleep. Perhaps I did. By 2.30AM I had the gearbox back in, the swinging arm connected, the rear wheel on and was reaching for one of the tool boxes when I saw something that made my heart sink. There, sitting on the floor, was a little part called the clutch pressure plate cup. It may be small but it's mighty. It sits in the middle of the clutch and the clutch rod pushes against it. Without it the clutch won't work. I slunk off to bed.

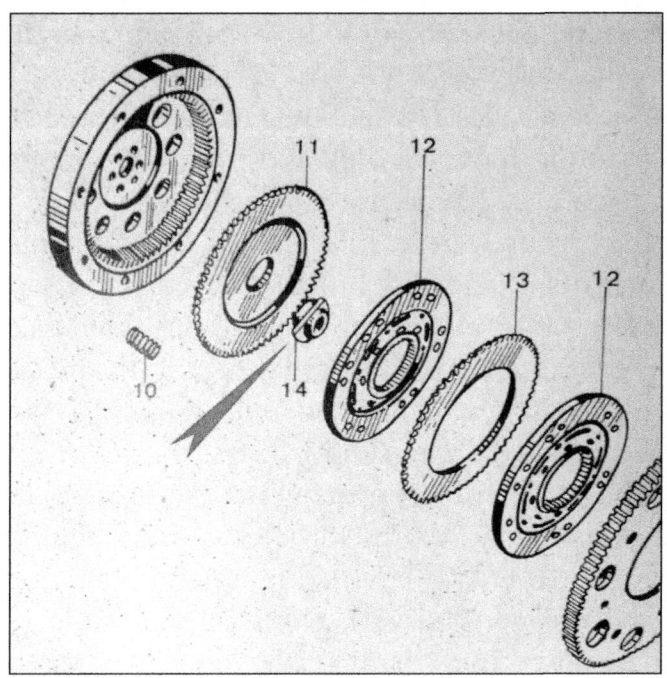

I slept deeply, but not for long. By 6AM I was back in the garage ripping into the Guzzi. Although I still had to remove the same old bits, I found that I didn't have to completely remove the gearbox. I was able to unbolt it, slide it back, sideways, and up, giving me just enough room to put the pressure plate cup in its rightful place. By breakfast time the bike was road-ready.

It started. It ran. The clutch disengaged when it was supposed to and engaged nicely when I let the lever out. It no longer created unexpected slack. Success. Although it's low speed carburation needed some work at anything above an idle the Eldorado was smooth and powerful. The gears and clutch worked as they should. I was soon rocketing along, relishing the crisp performance and the meaty sound from the Mistral exhausts. I almost wrote silencers there, but that would be a misnomer as they don't do much silencing.

After a few miles I turned around and headed home. I wanted to smooth out the idle and there were panniers and racks to install. As I accelerated up a long hill, I felt a slight judder from somewhere in the rear, accompanied by a disturbing rattle. I slowed, but all seemed smooth again. A little further on it happened again. This time I could tell there was definitely something happening in the rear drive box. I limped the remaining few miles home.

My first thought was "Did I forget to put oil in the rear drive?", but no, plenty of gear oil drained out, along with a disturbing quantity of metal flakes and chunks. The magnetic filler bolt was covered in small fragments of steel and the oil was spotted with chips of aluminum. If a few, well-chosen expletives tainted the air, I'm sure you can understand.

It's at times like this I find myself looking over at my more modern bikes, thinking, 'why don't I just make do with that instead, or better yet, buy a new Honda and to heck with these older bikes'. But much as I admire the efficiency and reliability of modern bikes, they just don't thrill me as much as the older ones. Call me irrational if you like. I set to work once again.

The problem was easy to identify. Two of the bolts that hold the bevel gears in place had chosen that moment to work themselves loose. As the bolt heads started to protrude, they had ripped through the webbing on the inner case, showering the internals with chips of aluminum, until the bolt heads parted company with the threaded bits and started rattling around on their own. How it could happen is anyone's guess. The bolts are secured with tab washers and should never have been able to work free. Why it happened then, after almost one hundred thousand road miles is a mystery. I was just glad it had happened close to home and not down some isolated road in the middle of nowhere.

Once I'd flushed out all the stray metal, I inspected the bevel gears. Astonishingly they were undamaged. No chips, no missing bits – nothing. They looked as good as new, or at least as good as one could reasonably expect after all those miles. I checked the bearings. They too seemed unfazed by the event. The case was a different story. The interior webbing was an ugly jagged mess. I looked for cracks or serious structural damage but could see none. I could live with ugly.

I drilled out the broken bolts, re-tapped the holes and reassembled the drive box, using good tab washers and copious amounts of thread-locker. With the wheel back on and new gear oil and moly in the drive, I gave it a spin. Smooth as silk. No nasty grinding or crunching noises at all.

With everything stitched back together I started the

Eldorado and took it for a quick spin around the block. Other than not wanting to idle on the right cylinder, which I eventually traced to a manifold gasket leak and a partially blocked idler circuit channel, everything seemed to be working well.

I dropped my friend Phil an email:

"Do you want to meet for lunch tomorrow? Haliburton? About 12ish?"

"Sure. Eldo?"

"Yep".

Haliburton is about equidistant between where Phil lives in Ancaster and where I live. It would be roughly 175 miles each way for both of us, although I got the better part of the deal. Phil had to navigate around the urban chaos of Toronto, while I had country roads the whole way.

If you're keyed up for another tale of roadside disaster, I'm sorry to disappoint you. The Eldorado behaved flawlessly and was running so well that Phil and I even explored a few back roads together before parting company again for the journey home.

Back on the road, at last

The newly rebuilt engine is very slightly smoother that its former 949cc self, but I do notice a fraction less torque on long, high gear hills. Obviously, those were early days, but things were looking good. I was delighted to have my Eldorado back in road-worthy trim and ready for some new adventures.

A few days later I decided that I now trusted the Eldorado enough that a good long shake down trip was in order. I packed, repacked, then packed again, telling my wife that I was probably just going to explore a few roads in northern Ontario, and I would be back in three or four days.

Twenty-two days and almost nine thousand miles later, I rolled the bike back into the garage. I'd got side-tracked. I'd ended up at the Arctic Circle in the Yukon Territory. You can read about it (and a couple of other trips) in my book "*Eldorado to the Klondike*".

AUTOMATICALLY RIDING

My 1976 Moto Guzzi Convert had languished in the garage all winter, quietly dripping ATF fluid from a little drain hole beneath the clutch housing into a shiny metal tray. By the end of the winter perhaps a third of a cup of the clear red lubricant had accumulated. In a perfect world it wouldn't leak – but when have any of my bikes been perfect? Put it down to Guzzi character if you like, but the reality is, when I had the bike apart to replace a worn-out clutch, I failed to order the correct oil seal and 'O' ring, so I'd put it back together knowing it would still leak. I'm not a careful mechanic. Never have been. And that's not likely to change at this stage of my life.

Minor, irritating drips notwithstanding, the Convert was ready to roll and so was I. Ontario was scheduled for its third 'stay home' Covid lock-down and I had just made the mistake of listening to Bob Segar singing *'Roll Me Away'*. For me, at least, he perfectly captured that desperate, almost painful aching need to ride, and keep on riding. I was spiritually with him as he *'rolled across the high plains, deep into the mountains'*. I decided right then that I would roll me away in the morning. I packed my tools, my lithium jump-starter and my rain gear in the panniers and checked and topped up the ATF tank. The bike was ready. The weather promised to be mild. I could hardly wait for daybreak.

Much as I would have liked to, I couldn't head for the mountains, and with the lock-down due to start the next day, I had to be home by nightfall, so I would do the next best thing: I would ride north through Ontario's rocks-and-lakes country to the southern edge of Algonquin Park. There, I knew, I would find quiet roads, still lakes and endless forest. Places where, when you stop, there is no sound other than the drone of Spring Peepers in the marshes, the hum of recently awakened insects, and the quiet lapping of tiny wavelets through the sedges at the lake shore. The region doesn't have the terrifying grandeur of towering mountains, but the gentle roll of the forested hills and the vast expanses of calm blue water are soothing and restorative.

1976 Moto Guzzi Convert

I had it in my mind to make a short video about the unexpected joys of riding an automatic motorbike. In the years that I've owned the Convert, I've heard numerous people express the opinion that for them, changing gears is an integral part of the whole motorbike riding experience. They argue that it's part of the skill set - finding that perfect balance between gear, clutch, and throttle through curve and over hill - listening to the rise and fall of the engine and exhaust note, matching speed and revs to the terrain. I get it. I really do. Four of the five bikes currently in my garage have gears, and they see a lot of road miles. Yet, there is something equally wonderful about riding automatic bikes. It is different, certainly, but, to me at least, equally satisfying and engaging. So, if you haven't done so already, do yourself a favour and beg, steal, or borrow a gearless motorbike and take it on a good long ride. No, not a quick spin around the block on your mate's Yamaha Vino Scooter – I mean a 'real' ride with hills, corners, traffic, and many, many miles. You might find it's a heck of a lot more entertaining than you imagine. You might even find you're Converted if you'll excuse the pun.

There is never much traffic heading north after crossing Highway 7 – the main road between Ottawa and Toronto. This is a land of forests, lakes, swamps, and rocks, with little human habitation. On this day, even though a cool sun was lighting the sky, the bare trees and exposed rock cuts made the world seem desolate and empty. There was no traffic to bother me. Occasionally I would see a pickup or car pass in the other direction, but for almost the whole time I was riding north, there was nothing in my mirrors and nothing ahead.

I was riding familiar roads until I turned on to the Old Barry's Bay Road, just north of Combermere. As I rode along between the tall poplar and spruce trees, which grow almost to the edge of the pavement, I could see an occasional flash of blue. Not too long ago, Rockingham Creek (Byer's Creek in some references) was used by local lumber companies to float logs from the harvest areas to the Madawaska River and from thence to the sawmills. To avoid some bends in the creek where the logs would jam, a wooden chute was built. This has been restored within the 'Crooked Chutes Park' – the water scenically flowing along the trough then plunging ten feet into the pool below. So, of course, I had to stop and look.

You would expect such a scenically attractive place to be crawling with people, and indeed, I suspect it would be on a sunny Sunday in summer. On this cool spring morning, though, it was deserted. I pulled the Convert into the parking lot, carefully choosing a spot where the sodden gravel had a hope of supporting the bike's weight on the side stand, shed my gear and went for a little walkabout. It truly is a lovely place. A wooden foot bridge spans the upper rapids, the crystal-clear water racing by, inches below your feet. The narrow wooden log slide diverts some of the stream's flow and spills scenically into the rocky pool below. I spent a happy few minutes wandering around before the urge to be riding again possessed me and I headed back out onto the road.

Crooked Chutes Park

A few miles further on I hit the brakes (note how it's spelled folks – it's brakes, not breaks!![2]) as I'd seen a front garden grotto I just couldn't pass by. Garden shrines to the

---

[2] *One of my internet forum pet peeves.*

Virgin Mary are fairly common in eastern Ontario. Actually, they're common wherever there's a sizeable Catholic population. Usually, they're the ubiquitous and totally tacky 'Mary in the Bathtub' – literally, a statue of Mary in half a vertical bathtub, the lower half dug into the ground. Occasionally, instead of a bathtub, a concrete Romanesque arch, a faux stone grotto, or an open wooden shelter will do.

The one that had caused me to stop and turn was the first of its kind I'd ever seen. A small, rather youthful Mary was standing on some fake rocks within a niche cut into the trunk of a felled tree. Most of the tree was gone but about five feet of the stump remained, nicely protected by an elegant cedar roof, while the base of the stump was enhanced by a pile of rocks.

What I assumed was a bible was lying on the rocks at the base of the plinth, although I didn't get off the bike to investigate. My interest in front garden iconography only extends so far.

Apparently, this part of Ontario was settled by people from the Kashubian district of what is now Poland, starting around 1858. And since many, if not most Poles are Catholic, it's not surprising that there are a few roadside shrines in the area.

The northern end of the Old Barry's Bay Road is a pleasant, quiet ride with plenty of curves and trees which seem to squeeze the road, opening, briefly, to give a glimpse of some small lakes – little more than large ponds, really – which occupy the valley to the west. There are few houses, mostly modern bungalows and the occasional farmhouse or small cottage from an earlier time, but they are well spread out and don't intrude on the pleasant riding. The old road ends abruptly at Highway 60 and it's a short jog west into Barry's Bay. For once, I managed to ride past the Tim Horton's on the main road without stopping for coffee, before turning up the Paugh Lake Road heading for the south side of Algonquin Park.

I had been expecting to hit gravel within a few kilometres of leaving Barry's Bay. Instead, I found flawless new paving and a big sign indicating that 3.1 million dollars were being spent on this road improvement. At first, I was a little disappointed, but the road was so pleasant that I soon found myself happily drifting along, rather pleased with the delightful, smooth ride. As I rode, I was busy with a monologue into my helmet microphone, explaining how I can't always expect the world to be organized for my pleasure, when I noticed that there was still deep snow in some of the ditches.

No sooner had I adjusted my mind to riding on the

lovely paving, than it abruptly ended. There was a woman in a white car on my tail, so as soon as it was safe, I pulled over to let her go by, trailing a cloud of dust in her wake. It is one thing to be happy with the wheels squirming around on the loose sand and gravel, but quite another to be chewing on the dust thrown up from the car ahead. I gave a her a few seconds to get well in front then resumed my ride.

Where the winter snowbanks were protected by shadow, they stood three feet high, not that they bothered me at all. The gravel was loose and dusty but free of snow and ice and the Convert was performing its normal magic of gliding effortlessly along. In places the gravel gave way to sand, which is not my favourite road surface, causing the front wheel to skip around as it got caught in the deeper and looser material. My video camera was still running and my little bit of commentary at this point was, 'I'm just not very brave when it comes to roads like this. I like to take it easy, because I actually like to get to where I'm going, and if that means slowing down just a bit, so be it.'

I find some riders tend to crank up the speed when the going gets rough. That may work for some people on some bikes, but not for me. I have no pretentions to off-roading skills, but so far at least, have managed to stay upright on unpaved roads by taking my time and reading the road surface ahead.

After a while I arrived at a bridge across a narrows between two lakes. I hadn't realized it at the time, but the bridge was crossing a sluggish section of the Bonnechere River which drains the southern edge of Algonquin Park and the Madawaska Highlands. The bridge itself was nothing to get excited about – just a slab of pavement between two guard rails – but to either side was calm, clear water edged with forest, and silence. I stood for a few minutes looking out over the blue water. I was still wearing my helmet, and since I've got into the habit of talking to myself, the camera recorded me saying 'I'm not exactly holding up traffic standing here'. During the whole time I was relaxing and wandering around, not a single vehicle passed in either direction.

A little further on, the 'main' road swung to the right, heading for Round Lake, but I turned left up the Basin Depot Road. In the heyday of logging, Basin Depot was a self-contained community with a post office, blacksmith's shop, and accommodation for nearly one hundred workers. Now, apparently, only two buildings remain – a log cabin and a warehouse. I say 'apparently' because I couldn't find out for myself.

As I headed down the road, the potholed and muddy road surface soon turned to old slush and snow, and it was clear the road hadn't been ploughed that winter. The sun had yet to fully penetrate the canopy of trees, shading four or five inches of wet, punky white stuff obscuring the road surface. One or two trucks had been through, but even where the road was free of snow, the gravel was so sodden that riding would have been tricky and dangerous. I pulled to the side at a delightful pond and, once again, sat quietly for a while, relishing the stillness of the day. A braver person might have ventured further, but in these infrequently travelled areas, a single 'whoops' could quickly become a life-threatening situation. I decided that discretion was the better part of valour and turned around.

If I was disappointed not to have been able to proceed further, that feeling soon evaporated. It was a stunning day – sunny, but not blindingly so, cool, but not chilly – a perfect day for riding. Following the road around Round Lake – as the name suggests, a roughly round lake about four miles in diameter – then down the Bonnechere Valley to Golden Lake then Eganville, I drifted along quietly curving, paved roads, punctuated by glorious views across the water. Somewhere along that stretch I'd left the rocky, forested hills of the Canadian Shield behind and entered a more benign landscape of flat pastures and grey, limestone rock. Deep in the past, almost five hundred million years ago, countless trillions of microscopic creatures living in an ancient tropical sea, had died and their corpses drifted to the bottom, gradually forming the Ordovician limestone rocks that lie exposed in this part of the Bonnechere Valley. At Forth Chutes, the Bonnechere River plunges over a series of steps in the naturally, horizontally bedded rock, creating a delightful series of small waterfalls. The nearby Bonnechere Caves are a local tourist attraction, but were closed because of the pandemic, but the parking lot was open and empty, so I parked the bike and spent a few happy moments watching the crystal-clear water racing by.

It might have been there, and it could have been when I'd stopped for a sandwich break a few miles back, but at one of those stops I left my selfie-stick behind. That's no great loss, you may be thinking. After all, how many glamour shots of some almost seventy-year-old guy next to some old clunker of a Moto Guzzi does the world need? But it was a particularly good one, with swivels and fittings which allowed me to attach any of my cameras, and a small, surprisingly stable tripod. It was a handy, well-made, multi-purpose tool, the loss of which I instantly regretted.

On the way home, on the pleasantly curvy Narrows Lock Road I was loving the relaxed way the automatic Convert oozes itself along. Bend coming up – just ease off the throttle a little, there's just enough engine braking to take the edge off any speed and steady the bike for the corner. Once into the corner, just roll the throttle on and the bike wafts its way along with no need for clutching, jerky gear changes or other interruptions to smooth, effortless progress. The Convert may not be the fastest bike on the road by any stretch of the imagination, but with the right road (and that pretty much means all of them) and one's head in the right place, it is a joy.

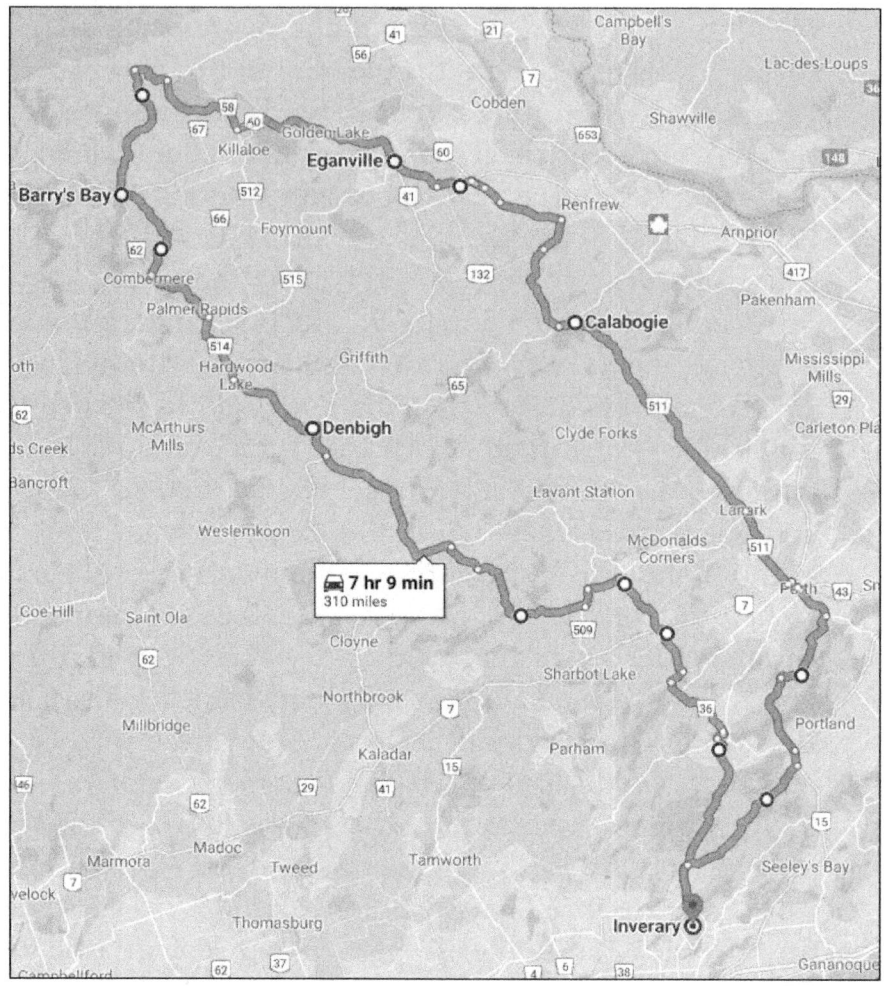

So Nick, if it is so good, why is the Convert sitting in the garage, tank off, with wires all over the place?

A few weeks later, I wheeled the Convert out of the garage for another little session of backroad exploration. I'd noticed a tiny thread of a road that I'd never ridden before, so I headed out for a short, holiday Monday afternoon ride. Since it was a sunny long weekend holiday there was plenty of traffic on the paved roads, but by the time I hit the unpaved Oak Flats Road they had all but disappeared, and by the time I turned onto the tiny, single-track Raymo

Road there was none. I suspect the Raymo Road is one of the many virtually abandoned sections of the Frontenac Colonization Road I've written about elsewhere. On the map it looks straight and uninteresting, but if you drill down, you can see that it twists and turns over every little rock outcrop and around every swamp while trying to maintain a steady northward path. There are still one or two old farmsteads, and signs that once there were a few more, but, as I was soon to find out, it's the kind of road you could lie down on for hours and not have to worry about getting run over.

The Convert was running nicely, and I was dribbling happily along with the engine barely above idle speed. And that was the problem. The charging system on Converts (and other Guzzis of that vintage) is notoriously weak and doesn't pump much charge into the battery at low revs. My battery was weak anyway, so the combination of low speed and the power drain from the headlight and auxiliary lights was sucking all its juice. Of course, I didn't know this. I happily pulled over next to a small pond and switched off to stretch my legs and take a few pictures. When it was time to remount and start again, I was greeted by faint clicks from the starter relay and nothing more.

At first, I didn't think much of it. This kind of truculent behavior from the Convert has happened before and I've always been able to get it started again. I'd got into the habit of always putting my lithium battery jump starter into the panniers before heading out on the road, but guess what? This time I'd left it behind.

I tried all the normal trouble shooting stuff. I checked fuses. I tightened battery terminals. I disconnected and re-connected wires on the off chance that some corrosion was affecting the flow of electrons. I checked that the spade terminal at the solenoid was attached and clean. I found nothing wrong. In the past I've been able to start old Guzzis by using a screwdriver to arc across the battery terminals, thereby bypassing switch, relay and all its associated wiring. I gave it a whirl, stirring up a few desultory sparks but not enough to turn the starter. Damn! I was out of tricks.

It was a beautiful day. The birds were twittering in the trees. The insects were humming – fortunately not too many of them the blood-sucking pestiferous kind – and all was quiet and peaceful. From the moment I'd turned on to the Raymo Road I hadn't seen another vehicle and throughout the whole time I was inspecting and fussing with the bike, nobody had been by.

Eastern Ontario is full of 'black holes' where there is no cell phone service, so I was shocked and surprised to find that a couple of bars of service were showing. I considered calling the Canadian Automobile Association rescue who would have turned up eventually, but since I wasn't too far away, I decided to give my good friend Norm a call.

"Hi Norm. Are you busy?"

"Nope. Just out in the garage. What's up?"

"The darn Convert won't start. Battery's dead"

"Where are you? Should I bring the trailer?"

I sent him a screenshot of my exact location on Google maps and walked back to sit on a pleasantly rounded bedrock outcrop overlooking the pond. It would take him a few minutes to wash up, attach the trailer to his car and hit the road.

Passing the time wasn't hard. In the spring, the small ponds and wetlands of the Canadian Shield are crawling with life, and I was content to sit back and watch it. The air was full of dragonflies, hawking back and forth snatching mosquitoes and deer flies out of the sky, helping keep me free from having my blood drained. I watch as a six-inch-long leech swam by, glad that my feet were firmly ensconced in my boots and not trailing in the murky water. Leeches have an incredible ability to home in on anything that might help them satisfy their lust for blood. Once, while launching a canoe into a northern lake, we'd seen leeches streaming from all directions as they detected the presence of fresh meat. It was enough to make your skin crawl.

Fortunately, my blood wasn't being offered to the denizens of the Canadian wilds and I was able to sit, quite contentedly until Norm arrived, a mere forty-five minutes after I'd called. His was the first (and only) vehicle to appear.

Norm had brought his jump-starter but after fiddling around with it for a few minutes, we conceded defeat and hoisted the bike on to the trailer.

The Convert is still sitting in my garage in disgrace. I have the tank off and the wiring exposed, and it's waiting for me to summon the energy and enthusiasm to go through the laborious process of thoroughly checking the wiring and replacing whatever needs replacing. I can't blame the bike though, and don't bother saying snarky and uninformed comments about Italian electrics. Before I got it, the bike had been completely rewired. I'm no expert, but I can see that there were some daft things done which, even to my untutored eye, were problems just waiting to happen. I need to move the main harness around so it isn't being flexed every time I turn the bars, and I should replace the starter relay as I suspect it may be part of the problem.

Eventually the Convert will be back on the road. It really is a magic bike to ride and has decades of life and countless miles left.

1986 SUZUKI CAVALCADE LXE[3]

When most people my age are quite sensibly looking at smaller, lighter motorbikes, as knees start creaking and backs ache, in the spring of 2020 I headed in the opposite direction, adding one of the largest, lardiest, and some might uncharitably say, ugliest motorcycles ever made to my garage.

Roll forward and take a bow, Suzuki Cavalcade, hustle your 34-year-old, chrome laden, 870lb (62stone) mass over this way so we can take a good look at you. Don't worry about that scratching noise; it's just your twin radio masts grazing the garage ceiling. Ignore that unkind heckling from the back row. You may not be a contender for the Banbury run or drool the contents of your sump across the garage floor in the time-honoured fashion, but as far as I'm concerned, despite your relative youth, you deserve a place in the pantheon of classics and some space in my garage. Indulge me for a moment and I'll explain.

Ever since I'd sold my Suzuki Burgman 650 scooter to pay for engine and gearbox repairs to my Moto Guzzi Eldorado, I'd been regretting it. The Burgman had been spectacularly good for two up touring, and I'd been on the lookout for a replacement ever since. None of my Guzzis

---

[3] *First published in 'RealClassic' magazine V.204, April 2021*

fit the bill. We are full sized people. For two up comfort and the distances we ride, a bike needed a big, stepped seat so Christine didn't have to look at the back of my head, plenty of luggage space for camping gear, enough power to be comfortable at highway speeds, and it had to be cheap. Another Burgman was certainly a possibility, but increasingly I found myself attracted to the big, lazy touring rigs from the nineteen eighties: bikes like the Yamaha Venture Royale, the Honda Goldwing Aspencade and the Kawasaki Voyager. That bikes of this vintage also happened to be right at the bottom of the price curve didn't hurt.

I soon discounted the Hondas. Although they were plentiful, the ones available were either completely worn out or absurdly expensive, and anyway, they did little for me - too common, too ordinary. The in-line engines of the Kawasakis didn't interest me much either, and any Venture I pursued turned out to be wretched or sold already. Then the Suzuki Cavalcade turned up.

1986 Suzuki Cavalcade

I vaguely knew that Suzuki had briefly entered the luxury touring barge fray in the mid-eighties, but I'd never seen one in the flesh. A quick search of the internet suggested that even though they had only been imported in small numbers, (700 in Canada, 7500 in the US, a handful in other countries) the consensus was that they were reliable, comfortable, and massively overbuilt, with the largest displacement engine (1360cc, 16 valve, DOHC V4) and the highest purchase price of all the big cruisers of the time.

It took Suzuki only four years to realise it wasn't going to beat Honda in the Goldwing stakes and pull out of the competition. Considering the quality and features they built into these Cavalcades, my guess is they were losing money on every one. It was an orphan, an ugly duckling, a monstrous tacky oddball, so of course, I was smitten.

The first owner had meticulously maintained and lavishly cleaned it. I doubt whether it had ever seen rain. I bought it from its second owner who'd promptly failed his riding test and parked the bike without putting any significant miles on it. The odometer showed just over 38,700 kilometres: less than 1200 kilometres a year since it left the factory, yet the carbs weren't gummy, nothing was rusty, and everything seemed to work.

It's a reasonable expectation that any 34-year-old motorbike is going to have its share of issues, and since I was feeding close to the bottom of the barrel, I wasn't expecting perfection. Incredibly, the list of horrors I encountered was minuscule. There's a small lever to the right of the passenger seat. This connects by cable to a spring-loaded rail which allows the top box and passenger seat back to move fore and aft. The lever is broken but the top box can still be moved by reaching underneath and activating the rail by hand. There should be a vanity mirror built into the top box. The little plastic legs on the mirror mount have failed. I won't be bothering to fix that. Initially the battery fluid level light was staying on (yes, it has one of those). Through the knowledge of the Worldwide Suzuki Cavalcade Owners Club (FB), I was able to send a query and got the response that the green wire at the battery should go to the positive terminal. The previous owner had attached it to the NEG terminal in error. And that's it. Everything else: the Radio/CB/Intercom system, the cruise control, the self-levelling suspension, the pneumatic passenger seat pad control, all work exactly as the manufacturer intended.

Starting is simple. Pull the choke lever open, pull in the self-adjusting hydraulic clutch, turn the key and the dash displays a very quick, basic systems check. There are no fuel taps to fuss with or carbs to tickle. The big V4 starts instantly on the button, the hydraulic valve adjusters do their work and the engine settles into a fast idle. Within a few moments you can close the lever, clunk into first gear, and roll away.

Because of its weight, at first the Cavalcade feels a little ponderous, and in truth, low speed turns are best taken with care. Once moving though, most of that weight disappears. Make no mistake, you still know you are on a very large motorcycle with acres of dashboard and fairing ahead of you, but the wide handlebars and the neutral, 'standard' riding position feel normal, and the bike feels controllable.

As one would expect from a big tourer, it's smooth and effortless on the highway. There is never a sense that the engine is working hard and the 180-degree crank produces a pleasing feeling – enough that you know there's an engine down there somewhere, even if it's not immediately obvious where. Rolling the Suzuki on in any gear produces an intoxicating, drama free increase in forward speed and a healthy, muted roar. Add a passenger and there is no noticeable difference in performance. It reminds me of the 1960 six-litre V8 Dodge Polara I had for a while. Its lazy motor barely breaks a sweat, even when asked to hustle.

Bikes like these were never designed for twisty roads, traffic congestion or filtering. At 43 inches across the mirrors, you're not going to be wiggling your way between the cars to the head of the line. They are about as suitable to tiny back roads as the Polara. They were designed for crossing continents; for saddling up in the morning and only stopping when the fuel tank is getting empty, and the rider's stomach is rumbling. Then doing it all over again, day after day, after day.

With such a mass underway and a 66-inch wheelbase, not surprisingly, it's not exactly what you might call flickable. When I first started riding it, I did find that it was a bit of a handful. Perhaps I was being too timid. I expected it to flop into the corners and must fight it. As the miles have accumulated, I have grown accustomed to the beast and now throw it around like a lightweight. OK, that may be a slight exaggeration, but now I just ride it and am only conscious of its considerable mass during slow speed maneuvers. It's not a bike for beginners perhaps, but it is entirely manageable once you've grown accustomed to its weight and surprisingly easy to ride smoothly. Indeed, with its rubber mounted engine and shaft drive, smoothness is the primary defining characteristic.

Once rolling, those fat tires, the soft pneumatic suspension and all that weight soak up road irregularities like an old Bentley. It really is easy to cover massive distances with virtually no effort. Shortly after I got it, I rode a 300 mile loop on a day when the thermometer struggled to reach double digits Celsius. The huge windscreen and wide bodywork did such a good job of keeping me out of the wind that I was only slightly chilled by the time I got home, and I was entirely free of the stiffness and discomfort that can accompany a long ride.

Given the high specifications of the bike, I was expecting linked brakes, as both its main competitors: the Yamaha Venture and the Honda Goldwing, offered linked brakes by the mid-nineteen eighties. Nevertheless, the Cavalcade's hydraulic triple disks (2x11inch front, 11.8-inch rear) do a fine job of slowing the beast. They need to be good too. Add a couple of human-sized individuals and all their gear, and those brakes are slowing almost half a ton.

It's a big bike (did I mention that already?) that seems custom made for someone my size. The seat height is 31.8 inches, yet I can easily flat foot it, and the rubber mounted foot pegs are exactly where they should be: directly below my knees. Those Suzuki folks thought of everything – even the foot pegs are adjustable to three positions – heck, even the passenger footboards are rubber mounted and have two positions.

You might think that getting such a monster on to its centre stand would be virtually impossible, but once again

Suzuki's clever engineers thoroughly thought it out. The stand has a robust, fold out lever: simply flick it out with your toe, stand on it while holding one of the passenger grab bars, and press forwards and down. Voila, the bike rolls backwards and without much effort, the rear wheel is off the ground.

After 34 years, thousands of Cavalcades in use and countless owner miles, it's a reasonable expectation that any fundamental reliability problems with the big Suzuki have already reared their heads and become common knowledge. Fortunately, problems have been relatively few. Over the years, some people experienced issues with the cast aluminum fork brace which has been known to crack at the mounting bolts. Since I knew that my Cavalcade would be spending time heavily loaded, I opted to be proactive and bought and installed a new, beefy billet brace, supplied at very reasonable cost by Cademaster Tracy at Palomino Manufacturing in Kansas. It fit like a glove.

There is also a plug in the secondary drive (the bevel gears which transmit power from the gearbox to the drive shaft) which, if it's not doing its job properly, can allow gear oil to flow from the secondary drive into the drive shaft tunnel. Obviously evacuating the gear oil from the drive isn't a good plan, and rear end lock ups have been known to occur once it runs dry. There is a replacement plug available, but since it's already been done (most have), I'll stick to checking the fluid levels regularly. Other than that, they seem indestructible. Stators, fuel pumps and water pumps will die, but replacements are readily available and easy to change.

As of the time of writing, I've added over 10,000 trouble-free miles to the clock, and, with one noticeable exception, the Cavalcade is living up to the Japanese motorcycle reputation of reliability and ease of use. This is a good thing. Any look behind the panels reveals a multitude of wires, tubes, switches and pumps, which do all kinds of complicated things I don't understand. This is not a bike I'll be taking out of cell phone range into the Canadian wilds as (actually, I would, and did! – see below), despite the comprehensive toolkit, roadside fixes are almost certainly out of the question. I wouldn't have a clue where to start.

Niggles? When I first got the bike, sometimes a press on the starter button was greeted with silence. It's a known issue caused by a sub-standard clutch switch. Soon after I got the bike, during a three day, thirteen hundred mile spin up to northern Ontario, starting gradually became more erratic until the darn bike wouldn't start at all. It took both the clutch and starter switch apart and cleaned them to no avail. Let me tell you, bump starting a fully loaded behemoth like this isn't an everyday pleasure, but it started willingly enough with a bump, and I was able to ride home. Fortunately, there is a permanent fix. A new high-quality switch uses hydraulic pressure from the clutch to open the electrical feed to the starter. It works flawlessly.

The top of the windscreen was right across my line of sight. I adjusted it down half an inch or so, but I could still do with trimming an inch off the screen. And it's a heavy bike. Perhaps I mentioned that, so moving it around in the garage can be tricky. I never thought the day would come when my Guzzi Eldorado would feel like a lightweight, but compared to the Cavalcade it's lithe, light, and sporty. The old girl doesn't need to worry though, I won't be consigning her to the cobwebs any time soon.

Legend has it that Suzuki spent a lot of time researching the requirements of the long-distance touring crowd while developing the Cavalcade and poured a huge amount of effort into the project, only to be beaten out at the showroom. This is a genuine shame as the engine is an absolute gem, with huge amounts of usable, smooth power and a surprising amount of character.

I'll willingly concede that the Suzuki Cavalcade isn't to everyone's taste. Its styling and dimensions are… unconstrained. It is the epitome of the unbridled excess of the eighties and is very much a product of its age. The styling is so completely, excessively eighties, right down to the CB, the cruise control, the absurd amount of chrome and the dirty-blonde and brown paintwork of which, against my better judgement, I've become absurdly fond. As my wife pointed out, the only thing that would have improved the factory paint job would have been if the brown panels had been fake woodgrain. I hope she was joking.

As a two up, long distance tourer it excels. On longer rides Chris has had to battle falling asleep, the passenger accommodation is so comfortable. While it wouldn't be the best choice to muscle out of the garage for a quick nip down to the shops or a half an hour spin to the local pub, if you have a continent to cross, a passenger to haul, and want to arrive fresh and unflustered, this may be the perfect bike to choose. That low mileage, well maintained, massive touring bikes of this vintage are also ridiculously cheap, is the icing on the cake.

DO IT WHILE YOU STILL CAN!

Back in July 2020 I had headed north on my 1986 Suzuki Cavalcade for a quick trip up to northern Ontario to experience whether I liked riding the big, bloated tourer on long trips and to visit the Abitibi Canyon. That trip was cut short by my own stupidity. I'd forgotten to check the condition of the tires and half-way through realized that the rear tire was bald. I scuttled home in the pouring rain, experiencing some irritating, almost show-stopping electrical issues on the way. If the suspense is killing you and you simply must read the full story, I wrote about it in my book *"Riding in the Time of the Plague"*.

With a new rear tire installed and the troublesome electrical gremlin evicted, my thoughts once again turned northwards. The weather forecast promised a spell of warmish weather, and since the leaves in our area were just showing the first signs of turning, I figured that the cooler temperatures further to the north would mean that the leaves would be spectacular. I wanted to ride up the Lake Superior coast, explore a couple of favourite inland routes and enjoy the mind-freeing experience of riding quiet roads through inspiring scenery. More importantly, a good friend had just announced that he'd acquired an old Russian motorbike and sidecar. He'd even posted a couple of short videos showing him chuffing around his garden on it. I needed to see that bike. His house was on the way. I could cadge a meal and a bed for the night. A perfect excuse – as if I needed one. And there was one more destination I had in mind. A curious thing that had caught my attention while cruising the internet one day: Something a little strange and possibly a little intimidating – but more of that later.

The capacious hard luggage of the Cavalcade swallowed my camping gear, rain suit and extra clothes with room to spare. On my other bikes I usually have all kinds of misshapen objects strapped to the back with bungees and elastic netting, so it made a real change for my travel bike to be in stealth mode. Nobody could tell whether I was just heading down to the corner, or across the continent. Usefully, the side cases and top box were adorned with large, chromed, industrial strength locks, so I could safely park the bike and forget it, confident that my stuff would be intact on my return.

I didn't get my usual early start. It had cooled off during the night and although it was obvious that, eventually, it would eventually be a sunny day, patchy ground-fog was lying in all the hollows for the first few miles. A few days earlier I had attached a GoPro camera to my helmet with a small microphone on the inside, just ahead of my lips. I'm terrible at keeping notes and rely heavily on photographs as memory joggers, but if I don't stop and take any pictures, any thoughts and observations I had along the way tend to evaporate. With the mike and camera, I thought I'd be able to make little audio notes and observations as I rode along. Not that these impressions are of earth-shattering consequence – it's usually little things like, 'that thermometer at the real estate agent's office in Cloyne says it's 4 degrees' or 'just the tips of the leaves are turning on a few of the trees – I hope they're more impressive further north', or 'man, there are a lot of dead raccoons on the road this morning' – simple stuff like that that keeps the journey fresh in my mind.

The first hours of riding were certainly fresh. It was warm enough that there was no danger of frost on the roads, but the cool air eventually found its way into all the weak spots in my riding gear. Although the Cavalcade's windscreen and lowers kept most of the windblast off my body, the wind has a nasty habit of circulating around behind me, chilling me between the shoulder blades. My hands were well protected by the fairing and mirrors but eventually, even they started to cool off.

I have a Calvinist attitude towards heated gear. It still feels like cheating to escape suffering so easily, simply by plugging something in or switching it on. Nevertheless, choking back my masochistic tendencies, I pulled over, grabbed my heated gloves from the top box and plugged them in. The wires, which dangle over my knees are a bit of a nuisance, but that was easy to overlook as the gentle heat started to bring some life back into my chilled fingers. I must be getting soft.

With roughly four hundred miles of riding ahead of me, despite the initial chill I was confident that the gradually warming sun would soon have me stopping again to shed layers. Being slightly chilled is fine as long as you know things will perk up later – as indeed they did. By the time I'd run through the first tank of fuel at Eganville, I abandoned the heated gloves, stripped the padded liners out of my riding pants, shed a sweater from beneath my leather jacket, and rolled on up past Lake Dore, and north on the 'B' Line Road until I joined the Trans-Canada Highway just west of Pembroke. I realise these placenames won't mean much to many of you, but there are map geeks out there who like to follow every little twist and turn. You're welcome.

How many times have I ridden or driven along the

Trans-Canada Highway between Pembroke and Sault Ste. Marie? It must be dozens, but it hasn't completely lost its appeal. I still get pleasure from viewing the rolling, forested hills, and the glimpses of the broad Ottawa River every time the road descends from the uplands. Although it's the main road across Canada, it is perfectly normal to be able to ride comfortably along, within spitting distance of the speed limit for hours, without having to touch the brakes. I had set my cruise control 'at exactly the speed limit officer', the big V4 humming along quietly. Freed from the need to hold the throttle I could move my hands around to different positions on the handlebars (and sometimes not hold on at all), while I alternated my feet between the pegs, the forward crash bars, and the passenger boards. With such a big, stable bike beneath me, I could clamber around like a monkey, stretching any parts that were thinking of getting stiff. This is exactly the kind of effortless mile-guzzling riding these big, full-sized tourers were designed for and I was loving it.

Chalk River, Deep River, Mattawa – where I stopped for a quick coffee – North Bay, Sturgeon Falls and Sudbury all disappeared in my rear-view mirrors, barely slowing progress at all. My destination was a few miles past Espanola where my friend's recently acquired motorbike and sidecar awaited my inspection. I was hoping to dump three litres of old oil at his house and replace it with the new, fresh oil I had tucked away in my panniers. I hadn't had time to do the oil change before I left, and it was a few miles overdue.

My friend – I'll call him Jacob, since that's the first name that sprung to mind – is one of those guys who you occasionally cross paths with in an internet forum and just know you are going to like. Jacob and I had exchanged many emails before I met him and he turned out to be exactly as I had anticipated: quiet, competent, generous, and knowledgeable about many of the things that interest me – so, nothing like me at all. Even so, our friendship has stuck, and it is a rare event for me to be in the vicinity of his house and not stop by.

1989 DNEPR
(prior to BMW engine transplant)

After a little relaxation and a truly scrumptious meal prepared by his equally welcoming and delightful wife who, for no discernable reason I'll call Amelia, we ambled outside to one of his sheds to look at his newly acquired Russian prize. The 1989 2WD Dnepr 650 sidecar rig took up almost every inch of the diminutive shed and sat there looking purposeful and elegant in its livery of black and aluminum. With scabby paint on the engine castings and rust speckles on the exposed frame parts, it wasn't going to win any prizes for aesthetics, but after cleaning some congealed gunk from its carburetors, Jacob had worked his magic and had it running cleanly. Over the winter, he anticipates evicting the gutless and failure prone Dnepr engine for a freshly rebuilt (and hopefully much more trustworthy) BMW 750/5 motor. Knowing Jacob's excellent mechanical skills, I expect to see it running in the new year.

Changing the oil on the Suzuki Cavalcade was a five-minute operation. Jacob slid under the engine with a big socket wrench and asked,

"Do you have a new filter?" then gently chided me for not replacing it this time or the time before and extracted a promise from me that I'd be sure to do it next time. I will Jacob – honest! You might be thinking, 'what a jerk to leave Jacob to deal with all that old oil' and you'd be right, it was a bit of a dirty trick. In my defence, with multiple bikes of his own and access to proper disposal facilities at work, I knew I would only be adding to his own stash of used oil which would eventually get recycled.

Jacob had work in the morning, and not being one to linger, I was soon heading west again along the Trans-Canada Highway. Once again, it was a chilly start. Once again there was low-lying fog in the hollows, but it soon dissipated and by the time I reached the turn-off to Elliot Lake it had warmed up enough for me to shed some cold weather clothing.

It would take a skilled poet to adequately describe the astonishing colours of the northern maple forests in full fall display. As I rode north towards Elliot Lake the ribbon of immaculately paved highway was lined with trees displaying every shade of yellow, red and brown you can possibly imagine, the early morning sun illuminating whole hillsides vibrant with vivid autumn hues. The trees had been becoming steadily more impressive as I rode north and west but reached their zenith on this road in the oblique early morning sun. I'd muttered some nonsense into my microphone about God being an impressionist painter, daubing the hillsides with splashes from a comprehensive palette, and while it had seemed profound at the time, when I listened to it afterwards it sounded like gibberish. All I can suggest is that at some point in your lives, make a pilgrimage to see autumn in the Great North Woods. You won't regret it.

I've briefly described Elliot Lake in another collection of road tales, as a thriving retirement community which had emerged, phoenix-like from a slowly dying former uranium mining town. Nothing I saw this time convinced me that anything had changed. The lakeside park was still immaculately groomed with healthy-looking people jogging, cycling, or strolling along its paths. The grass along the side roads was scrupulously cropped, the parking lots at the grocery and hardware stores were huge, clean, and largely empty. Most of the vehicles I saw were relatively new and spotlessly clean. The place looked wholesome and prosperous.

If you looked closely, you might notice a disproportionately large amount of grey hair distributed around the healthy-looking folks, and rather fewer young and middle aged people than one might expect. Come to think of it, the whole place is a little too clean – a little too well managed. It started to remind me of one of those mysterious, idyllic worlds on *"Star Trek"* where everything is perfect – until the crew discover some grim and disturbing secret that keeps the population balance in check.

The number of minutes I've spent in Elliot Lake in the last twenty years can easily be counted on my fingers. I've bought gas, but otherwise have always just been passing through. But, when you've been sitting on a bike seat for a while, giving that enormous, convoluted human brain little to do beyond keeping the bike out of the weeds, it's bound to go off having little adventures on its own. As I left town I checked my mirrors, but since I couldn't see any grey-haired hordes of zombies racing up the road behind me, I assumed my imagination was getting the better of me and kept riding north.

Highway 108/639 runs almost straight north from Elliot Lake, through Mississagi Provincial Park to its junction with the Little White River Road. A municipal dump truck was lumbering up the road ahead of me, belching black smoke as it ground up the hills. There were plenty of opportunities for me to overtake, but as I was in no hurry, I hung well back and idled along, enjoying the stunning colours lining the road. Eventually the truck turned off towards the Quirke Lake Mine, the road narrowed, lost its white lines, and started to feel a little more remote. Whenever I stopped to take photographs, I was greeted with that awesome silence that surrounds you when you have made it beyond the constant background hum of the busy world of human activity. But in truth there wasn't silence. There was a faint rustling in the treetops, the tinkle of water making its way down some tiny stream, the peeping of small birds, the churring of angry squirrels and the snapping of twigs as some large animal made its stealthy way towards the unsuspecting rider. I'm just kidding about the last bit. I heard no such noises, but there's some part of our primeval monkey brain that's always got one ear cocked for sounds that might announce the imminent arrival of a predator.

Nothing emerged from the dark forest. You could spend a lifetime standing in the same spot with far less chance of being attacked by something with murderous intent than if you were standing in the entrance to Wal-Mart. I packed my cameras away and rolled on.

Highway 639 was completed in 1963 with almost no regard to the upland topography through which it passes. Instead of avoiding hills by taking a circuitous route, it cuts straight through, exposing the gnarly granite bedrock in almost constant vertically faced rock cuts. Where it crosses dips and valleys, the road has been built on huge berms of fill, lying well above the surrounding terrain. This makes it sound uninteresting, and indeed, for those looking to wear the chicken-strips off their tires they're out of luck, but it's oddly pleasant to see the bones of the country exposed so clearly.

Eventually the main highway ends at a T-junction. To the east, a minor road leads to Mount Lake, McErea Lake and the interior country beyond, but ultimately dead ends in the forest. To the west lies the delightful Little White River Road, leading back down to the Trans-Canada Highway at Iron Bridge. I turned left.

Just past the intersection the signs promised a bumpy and twisty road for 33 of the 40 miles to Iron Bridge. Cool! I was looking forward to seeing how the mighty Cavalcade would fare. I had ridden this road in the other direction a few years before on my old Guzzi and was curious to see how that experience would match riding my 'modern' bike.

Within less than a mile of turning the corner, you cross

a bridge, and from that point on, for the next twenty miles or more, the road sticks close to the river. The river winds a convoluted path through its broad valley, with plenty of bends, oxbows and dead channels, while the road takes a more direct path, never diverging far from the Little White. It's hard to imagine more pleasant and relaxing riding. With no traffic to worry about and delightful views of the river constantly present, it's captivating to ride slowly, sucking in the clean air, stopping occasionally to listen to the sound of the water rippling over the rivers stony bed, to dream of snagging brook trout from its pools. Not that I ever bother with fishing, but it's nice to imagine.

Along the Little White River Road

The road lives up the warning signs: its surface is poorly laid and full of frost heaves, with patches of loose gravel in the almost-constant corners. The Cavalcade handled it all with smooth equanimity. Occasionally a particularly rough section would rattle the plastic dash, but the suspension did a fine job of smoothing out the bumps, and the surprisingly adept chassis handled the corners without drama. The Cavalcade may not have the deeply cool factor of my 72 Guzzi, but it rolled along in a surprisingly enjoyable way.

I suppose there will be those who think that a twisty paved road like this must be ridden at 98%, like the sport-bike riding boneheads who tear up Mulholland Highway, but if so, I hope I'm not around at the time. I would have a hard time being a good Samaritan to some idiot who'd wrapped his bike around a tree or spun off into the river through his or her own stupidity and thoughtlessness.

Eventually I left the river behind, spun through the back end of Iron Bridge and rejoined the Trans-Canada highway heading east towards Sault Ste. Marie. It was still early in the day and although I had a vague idea of my itinerary, it was subject to change on a whim.

I'd had enough of the Trans-Canada by the time I reached Bruce Mines, and although it made little sense for making time and distance, I once again abandoned the highway for an old favourite of mine which headed north towards Rydal Bank – a place I'd lived in the distant past.

It's always intriguing to revisit old haunts, only to find that the places you thought you knew so well have morphed in your memory during the intervening years. The whole area was hillier than I remembered. Houses and farms weren't where I expected them to be. The landscape was better managed and less scruffy than I recalled. These were just changes in what I remembered, but real changes had also happened. Buildings I expected to be there were gone. The alignment of some of the hamlet's roads had changed. The two shoddy shacks Christine and I had once inhabited had been demolished.

I thought briefly about dropping in unexpectedly on our one remaining friend in the area, but decided against it, opting to take the 'short' way to the Soo[4] up the Plummer Road, part of an old colonization road built in the 1860s to attract settlers to the area and facilitate travel in the region.

After Rydal Bank the asphalt surface fizzled out and I was soon piloting the heavy Cavalcade along a hard-packed gravel surface. I was please to find that the bike wasn't the handful I'd expected, and even when I had to pass through some road works where the crew had repaired their excavation with truckloads of soft sandy gravel, the bike remained stable and controllable.

The gravel eventually ended, and I turned on to the narrow, paved Centreline Road heading briefly north towards Gordon Lake. This lovely lake is surrounded by high quartzite ridges, the bare rock gleaming in the midday sun. The surrounding forest was a riot of red, brown and yellow as the maple trees displayed their full glory. Despite its beauty though, I had another reason for being there. Long before Chris and I were married we'd sat together on a low rock at the water's edge, looking out over the reedy water. It had been a romantic moment in a romantic setting, and I was happy to park the bike for a few moments and think about how, miraculously, some forty-two years later, nothing has changed in our feelings for each other.

---

[4] The Soo – abbreviation for Sault. Ste Marie. Sault is French for jump – referring to the St. Mary's River rapids where the river leaves Lake Superior.

Romantic memory

A little further on the rocky hills surround the broad Sylvan Valley, dotted with small farms amid well-cared-for fields. Ever since I'd first seen them there decades before, I always looked for Sandhill Cranes picking frogs and seeds from between the freshly harvested crops. I was not disappointed. There was a whole flock of the tall, stately birds in the first field, but sadly, as soon as I slowed the bike at the field entrance, they all took flight in a flurry of gigantic wings. I had better luck in the second field and was able to spend a few joyful moments watching as they stalked around. The adults are grey, with brownish flight feathers and a red forehead, whereas the juvenile birds have uniformly buff-coloured feathers. It was interesting to see that, like teenagers everywhere, the young birds tend to hang around in groups looking gormless, while their parents get on with the serious business of filling their crops before the next stage of their southward migration.

I had been really looking forward to riding up the coast of Lake Superior from the Soo to Wawa. It's a trip I've done many times before and it usually excites and thrills me to see the massive lake spreading off to the horizon with the high, forested bluffs stretching off towards the east and north, but first I had to fill my fuel tank and replenish my empty stomach.

Back in the late nineteen-seventies when I lived in Sault Ste Marie, the 'Trading Post' just past 4th Line as you were leaving the Soo, was a gas station and general Canadiana knick-knack store where you could buy a chocolate bar, a pair of moccasins, a velvet picture of dogs playing pool, a faux Indian beaded belt, beef jerky, an orange hunting cap, a few fishing lures, regional maps and a wide variety of other useful and/or trashy items. I remember the place well. During my first Canadian winter, I learned that there is nothing, simply nothing you can do to control a four-wheel skid on freezing rain, as I drifted past the Trading Post, totally out of control. After I'd finally managed to stop the car, I ended up sitting outside under their porch while I waited for the grit trucks to go by and my nerves to settle.

Times have changed. The old Trading Post building is still there (or at least, I assume it's the same one), only now it's 'Hunter's Headquarters' selling guns, licences, ammo and accessories, as well as a handy sideline in fireworks and propane – an incendiary mix if ever there was one. And the place has massively expanded.

Nowadays the knick-knacks are available in the separate acid-green 'Totem Pole" (gifts and souvenirs) building, and behind them is a row of absurdly inappropriate, gaily painted faux 'western' false-fronted buildings selling burgers, fish, pizza, chips, and beer. They were the last place heading out of town so, you guessed it, I swallowed the lump of bile in my throat, ordered some chips and sat on a bench outside 'Frenchies Fish House' while insipid country music blared from a host of loudspeakers. The chips were good though.

Lake Superior is mind-bogglingly huge. You can only ever see tiny portions of it at any one time and I'm always searching for ways to describe its extent. Here is my latest. If you could somehow extricate the whole of Ireland (surface area 32,599 sq miles) from the European continental shelf and plonk it down into Lake Superior (surface area 31,700 sq miles), it would only be fractionally too large. Of course, if you were able to do that, the 2,900 cubic miles of water you spilled would cover the whole of North and South America in a foot of water - or so I'm reliably informed by Wikipedia. Hmm. Some days I'm not sure that wouldn't be a good thing.

Lake Superior

The weather was gorgeous, the bike was running beautifully, the scenery was as dramatic and scenic as ever and the traffic was light, but for some obscure reason, I just wasn't feeling it this time. There was nothing external I could put my finger on. Internally I was feeling buoyant and cheerful, so I couldn't even blame my mood. Perhaps I'd ridden that stretch of road one too many times, and it shouldn't be taken as a negative attitude towards a ride which, by any standard is inspiring and agreeable.

The Cavalcade romped on, cruise control engaged most of the time, flattening even the highest hills without any noticeable change in engine pitch or effort. As I rode towards Montreal River, I passed the place where, decades before, as a newly minted Canadian immigrant I'd almost crashed my Austin Mini. I know. An Austin Mini was a ridiculous choice of car for Canada, but I'd only been through one winter and hadn't yet fully internalized the requirements for comfortable and safe winter travel. I was still stuck in the British mentality which favoured running costs above all.

I was on my way back to the Soo from a mid-winter archaeological conference in Thunder Bay with my two large dogs sandwiched into the rear seat. The roads had been bare and dry when I started out, but as I passed through Wawa heading south, a storm had built over Lake Superior, and it was snowing steadily and accumulating fast on the road. I gingerly made it down the Montreal River Hill – a two-mile-long descent from the upland plateau to the Lake Superior shore – by keeping my wheels on the flattened, hard-packed snow where heavy transport trucks had passed. If I got out of the ruts, the tiny, ten-inch Mini wheels were difficult to control in the loose deep snow.

Having made it down the hill and across the river, I thought I was in the clear, but as I increased speed the wheels lost traction and in an instant, I was in a spin. Even now, years later, I can remember the sensation well. Everything seemed to happen in slow motion. The car spun through a complete revolution, then started on a second. In those first moments I was confused and disoriented, but as the car entered its second three-sixty, I was able to get the wheels heading in the right direction and as it straightened up again, gave a touch of throttle and astonishingly, was able to keep driving straight.

It's a good job there was no other traffic as I'd drifted right across the highway and was fully in the north-bound lane. Had a truck been coming the other way, the car would have been squished like a bug. The dogs barely even lifted their heads from their slumber.

Nothing that exciting or dangerous occurred to affect my progress north this time and it wasn't long before I was parking the bike at the Wawa 'Tim's' and heading in for a coffee and a sandwich. Because of restrictions in place to limit the spread of Covid-19, facemasks and social distancing were mandatory and many of the inside tables were roped off, but I was able to enjoy a few minutes off the bike, replenishing myself.

Time was marching on. I'd already ridden a good few miles but it was still too early to stop for the day. I decided that I would head for Chapleau (pop. 2000), a small railway town about eighty-seven miles to the east. I was unclear about my plans after that but assumed they'd resolve themselves after a decent supper and a beer or two.

Highway 101 between Wawa and Chapleau starts off scenically enough, with glimpses of Wawa Lake between the trees, high wooded hills, and towering rock bluffs. After a few miles though, the land flattens out and much of the ride is along a straight, well-surfaced road lined by endless forest. Some might find this tedious as it is undemanding, steady riding with no challenging corners or imposing views to engage the attention. I don't mind though – this vast country is what it is – and it's a mistake to expect it to be something it isn't. The very scale of the land is what I find engaging. In eighty-seven miles, you pass through zero communities, one or two huntin'/fishin' lodges barely visible from the road, and 'Shoals Provincial Park', now a non-operational park – victim of an ill-considered government cost-cutting blitz. And that's about it – no traffic lights, no traffic, no pubs, cafés, or shops. Just a big, empty road through the forest. I love it.

Unfortunately, I'd seriously misjudged my timing. I rolled into Chapleau, crossed the weirdly serpentine overpass which carries traffic over the railway bisecting the town, and headed for the LCBO[5]. Finding it was easy enough, I'd been there before, but to my surprise and disappointment it was closed. In horror I looked at my phone only to find that it was 6.15PM – I was just fifteen miserable minutes too late. Back on the bike, I scuttled a few streets over, desperately hoping that the 'Beer Store' didn't operate the same hours. Darn it, it too was closed. My last alternative was to find a licenced restaurant where I could fulfil my desire for both food and drink, but all the restaurants were shut up tight too – victims of anti-Covid restrictions. There was nothing else for it – it was going to be a dry, healthy night of gas station pizza and pop in the motel.

That evening, through the wonders of the internet, I chatted to my wife and to my Dnepr owning friend Jacob. Christine informed me that all our vehicle licence stickers were out of date. They had become due for replacement on

---

[5] LCBO: Liquor Control Board of Ontario. Government run booze store.

my birthday, but somehow it had skipped my mind so here we were, almost two months later, driving vehicles that could be pulled over by the police at any moment[6]. She could do nothing about it since all the vehicles were registered in my name. We could either chance it for a few more days, or I could rush home.

I didn't mention the licence debacle to Jacob, but I did say I was thinking about cutting my trip short to make the twelve-hour, 600+ mile ride home the following day. Wisely Jacob reminded me that I'd also curtailed my previous ride because of the bald tire, and I would kick myself afterwards if I did the same this time. He was right. The licence renewals could wait. I would proceed.

During the previous winter I'd been stumbling around the internet, dreaming of future adventures, when I came across a peculiar landform. I'd been researching the Otish Mountains in far northeastern Quebec, wondering if the newly constructed mine road extending inland from Lake Mistassini would be rideable on my old Guzzi when I spotted a reference to Mont Chaudron – an unusually shaped small mountain near the Ontario / Quebec border. It was a peculiar thing. In a heavily glaciated landscape of rounded knobs and low, forested hills, it stuck out like a miniature Devil's Tower. I filed the information away in a remote corner of my amygdala then promptly forgot all about it.

Why that portion of my brain was triggered while riding through the endless forests east of Wawa is anyone's guess. Perhaps, without the riding placing much demand on my concentration, some little neuron was rooting around

---

[6] *Little did any of us know that because of the Pandemic, a moratorium had been placed on renewing licence stickers.*

on its own and threw it up at random. That evening, after chatting with Christine and Jacob, I checked Google Maps, found the mysterious mountain, and formed a plan. I would ride the two hundred and fifty miles to the Quebec border in the morning, climb or scramble up Mont Chaudron if I had the stamina and skill, then, assuming I didn't break my neck or explode my heart, ride in the general direction of home until I was too tired to go any further.

Like an idiot, when I'd been buying my pizza at the gas station the previous evening, I'd not bothered to fill the bike. The young woman at the counter assured me they would open at 6AM, but when I arrived at about 6.02, I was promptly told they didn't start the fuel pumps till seven. Even though it was still completely dark, only just above freezing, and foggy, and a sensible person would have parked the bike and gone in to kill time over a cooked breakfast, I was soon heading east towards Foleyet, just over sixty miles away, where I knew there was another gas station.

I like riding in the dark, the Suzuki has terrific headlights, and with no insect pests floating about, I was able to lift my visor and ride through the night air without eye protection. Gradually the patchy fog started to rise as light appeared in the eastern sky, at first as a grey band over the horizon, turning to hazy pink as the sun started to claw its way into the sky. That's complete rubbish, of course. I know the earth rotates around the sun, and as far as we know, the sun doesn't claw anywhere, but it's not hard to see why people believed it was the other way around when you watch the dawn unfold.

I had been keeping a wary eye out for moose and other large fleshy things looming out of the forest, but it was almost light before I saw the first signs of life. A young wolf trotted unhurriedly across the road a hundred yards ahead of me and disappeared into the forest. A few minutes later, I caught a glimpse the rear end of a much larger wolf as he left the road, his unmistakable curved tail stretching out behind his lanky rear end. It's not unusual to see moose, bears, porcupines, skunks, and squirrels on or near the roads, especially at dawn and dusk, but wolves are a much rarer sight. I was feeling doubly blessed.

The general store in Foleyet was open and had fuel. For a small store in a remote hamlet, it was well stocked with hardware, food, fishing and hunting supplies and important stuff like toilet paper and dish detergent. If this shop was your only option for miles, you could get by.

By the time I reached the City of Timmins (pop 42,000) I was in serious need of some breakfast, so I pulled into the first Tim Hortons I saw, only to discover it was strictly a drive through. As I moved through the town, I was sorely tempted by proper restaurants which offered proper breakfast fare, but being a creature of habit, and cheap, I pulled into another Tim's in South Porcupine – the original gold mining core settlement around which the city developed.

The Tim's was doing a bustling drive-through trade while only a handful of people had opted to seat themselves in the interior. As I sipped my coffee and chewed into my 'sausage-breakfast-sandwich-on-a-homestyle-biscuit', even opting for the optional, plasticky hash-brown because I was starving, I noticed the fellow over by the window watching me.

Us humans are hard-wired to notice even the slightest subtleties of expression or manner, so it didn't take too many sips of my coffee before I was confident that this well-dressed, slightly overweight, middle-aged man was desperately eager to talk to me and was struggling to find an entranceway into conversation. If I'm riding my old Guzzi Eldorado I expect conversation. Even non-motorcycle people recognize it as an older bike, and since it's usually covered in strapped on bags and extra fuel containers, it provides an easy dialogue gateway for the curious. The Cavalcade, however, is virtually invisible. Unless you are a motorcycle geek it just looks like any other fully dressed tourer and there are no external clues as to whether I've just ridden from around the block or across the country.

After numerous glances my way and after steeling himself by getting another 'triple-triple'[7] and a sugar encrusted donut, he finally plucked up the nerve. In a voice far too loud for the situation, he blurted,

"MY DOG LIKES TO EAT GARBAGE".

It wasn't quite the opening line I was expecting, but we soon had a fine conversation going about his dog's weekly adventures, which involved ripping into, and redistributing the neighbour's trash which had been put out on the side of the road to be collected by the municipal truck.

By now my coffee and sandwich were gone, so before I learned any more about his, or his dogs' habits, I said goodbye, wished him a good day and headed back to the bike. As I got myself organized, I saw him watching me. I like to think he was wistfully dreaming of riding off on a big motorcycle himself, but I suspect he was still thinking about his dog.

I still had over a hundred miles to ride before I could exercise my hiking boots. With yet more fuel in the tank, a more comfortable feel in my own tank and a decent road

---

[7] Triple-triple: Coffee with three spoonfuls of sugar and three doses of cream....ugh!

ahead, I picked up speed a little and was soon devouring the miles, passing through Matheson and Virginiatown before arriving at my destination just after lunch time.

I didn't stop in Matheson this time, although I usually stop for a brief break at the Ontario Government historical plaque, more out of a ghoulish curiosity than from any need to refresh my memory of its contents. In a nutshell, while clearing land in the summer of 1916 by 'slash and burn', some smaller fires coalesced into one massive conflagration, which roared through the area killing two hundred and twenty-three people. There was no warning and no means of escape, except for the few who managed to board the Temiskaming and Northern Ontario Railway train or survived by sheltering in the waters of nearby rivers and lakes. It remains the largest loss of life through forest fire in recorded Canadian history.

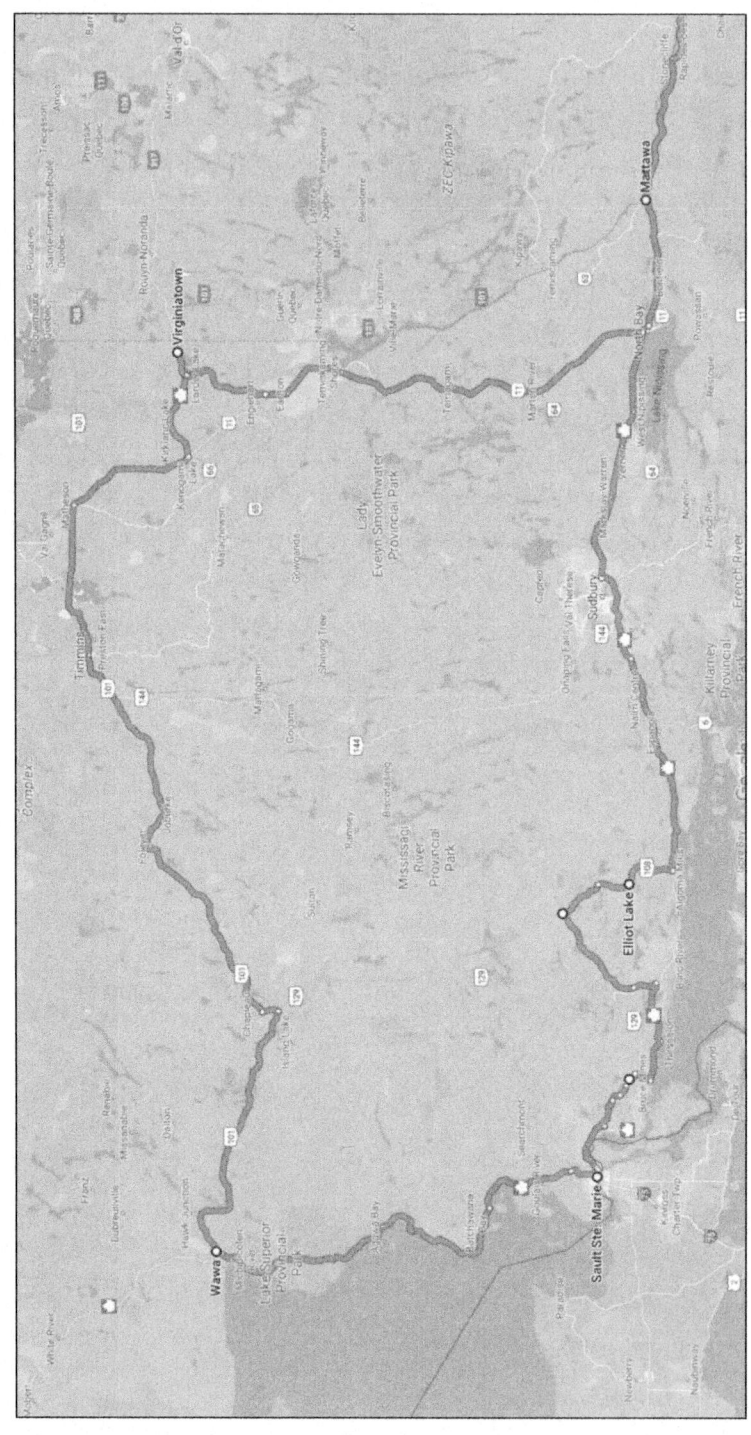

I had looked at the parking arrangements for Mont Chaudron on Google Streetview so I didn't have to hunt around for the start of the trail. Just a rough gravel pull-in provided room for vehicles while a narrow bush road led south through the bush toward the mountain. There was only a single car in the parking area when I arrived – a good sign as far as I was concerned. I parked the bike, stripped off my riding gear, locked it in the panniers and headed down the trail.

Almost immediately I was too hot. Air that feels cool when you're rushing through it at sixty miles an hour is quite a different kettle of fish when you're walking through it up a rough gravel track. I stripped off my thin quilted jacked and tied it around my waist. A few hundred yards further on, I pulled my sweater over my head and carried it. Sweat was beginning to bead on my forehead and I wasn't even half-way to the base of the climb.

Oddly, it's impossible to gain a decent view of Mont Chaudron from the first part of the trail. You have the feeling that there might be something bulky and looming behind the thick screen of trees but other than the occasional glimpse of bare vertical rock, there is no way to see its whole extent.

After about a mile, a sign indicated the real start of the hiking trail. I shed yet another layer, hung my clothes in a bush behind a sign, cursed myself for not changing my now sticky and sweaty jeans for shorts and ploughed on. A rough path led abruptly through thick forest gaining altitude quickly, the footing rapidly turning from a typical forest path of soil and roots, to jumbled rock talus. Close to the edge of the trees, an Australian Shepherd – the dog, not the guy – lurched around a rock towards me, straining on the end of his leash.

"Don't worry, he's friendly" said the young lady at the

other end of his rope, as he gave my hand a perfunctory lick.

"So am I" I said. "Did you go all the way up?"

"No, I had to turn back – it was too steep for me."

We exchanged a few more pleasantries before we went our separate ways. I'd been happy for a few seconds break from the climb, and as I continued upwards, I wondered what I was about to face.

Mont Chaudron (or Mount Cheminis)

By the time I was through the talus field and reached the base of the cliff my heart and lungs were operating at maximum speed, and I no longer had any doubt why the young lady had turned back. Ahead was a pitch of almost vertical rock which few dogs would be able to climb. Someone had provided a knotted rope, but even with the rope it was a daunting ascent.

Before I go any further – and frankly, I'm happy to take a break, from the exertion of climbing, even in retrospect – I suppose I'd better tell you a little more about this exceptional place. Mont Chaudron is an *inselberg*, an isolated 'mountain island' surrounded by much lower topography. The harder rock of the 'island' proved more resistant to glaciation, so while the ice sheets of the last ice age carved away much of the surrounding plain, the 527 metre (1729 feet) high Mont Chaudron was left as a protuberant hill rising abruptly more than 250 metres from the adjacent country. Its base emerges out of the surrounding forest in a steeply sloping tangle of blocky rock-scree containing everything from fist-sized gravel to boulders the size of a small car. Above the talus slope, vertical cliffs surround the oval mountain which is topped by a more-or-less level crown of forest.

On the world stage, Mont Chaudron doesn't rate as much above a pimple. It's no Matterhorn, Pikes Peak or even Snowdon – even many of the lesser peaks along the Pennines in England are higher – but in the generally level landscape where it resides, it is both unusual and outstanding. Such distinctiveness undoubtedly intrigued people for generations.

The French word chaudron means cauldron, which, I assume, refers to the hill's resemblance to an upside-down cooking pot. Although lying just on the Quebec side of the provincial border, in Ontario it is often referred to as Mount Cheminis – a name which may be derived from 'Shaman' or a place of healers or healing. Whatever the etymology of its names, I have little doubt it was well known and visited by First Nations people. It is easy to imagine it being used as the place for experiencing life-guiding visions or for making personal contact with the gods.

With some of my stamina and breath regained, I started the clamber up the steep rock face. The rope wasn't really necessary as there were plenty of well-worn hand and foot holds. In surprisingly little time I was making my way along the narrow path towards the lookout at the northern edge of the mountain, where a bare terrace of rock ended abruptly in vertical cliffs considerably higher than the ones up which I'd just climbed.

To say the view was outstanding barely does it justice. Far below, a carpet of many-hued forest, spotted with small lakes and dappled with cloud-shadows stretched out to the horizon. This was a perfect place for a good, long contemplative sit, but being a sweat-drenched restless person, I soon found the trail that rings the mountain top and carried on.

There is one piece of intelligence about the area which I hadn't known at the time, and had I done so, my feelings about the top of Mont Chaudron might have been very different. Rather than paraphrasing it, I'll render the information exactly as it appears in Wikipedia:

> "the body of a man, minus a head, two hands and a right foot was found on the top of Mount Cheminis. Nearby was a shotgun and an empty cartridge in the chamber. The clothes were 'city clothes,' not bush clothing. There was absolutely no identification, and nobody has been reported missing in the area since July, 1954."

and,

Quote from Le Progrès in July 1955:

"The body was found by three young people who were demarcating lots for the government. A rifle in which there was a perforated bullet and a bottle of alcohol were found on a newspaper dated July 5, 1954, some 30 feet from the corpse, who was wearing a gray town dress."

It's hard to know what to make of this. Was this poor man murdered and his head, hands and foot removed to prevent identification? If so, what was special about his foot, and why would his murderers make the tricky climb to kill him? By leaving him in such a prominent position, were they making a statement? If so, to whom?

If this was a suicide, as the booze bottle, newspaper and gun might suggest, what happened to his head and extremities? One might think they could have been carried off by animals, but it seems unlikely that any large carnivore would climb the vertical cliffs to make off with or consume the body parts. Perhaps the corpse was so deteriorated that the police simply didn't notice the small bones of the hands and foot. Could the skull have been shattered by a self-inflicted shotgun blast and the pieces scattered into the vegetation, unnoticed and unrecognized? Did someone take bits as souvenirs? The questions are endless. I suppose by now any physical evidence collected at the scene will have long since disappeared. It's a cold case that may never be solved.

The rough, poorly defined path rings the mountain top, brought me back to the cliff and rope. As far as I was able to tell, this is the only way up and down unless you are a skilled rock climber with the appropriate amount of safety equipment.

Looking down the pitch was daunting. The hand and foot holds have become well-smoothed by other hikers over the years, and while going up was relatively painless, turning around to face the rock, searching for a foothold, my body hanging over empty space with nothing but angular granite blocks to break any fall was intimidating. The stupid twenty-something who still inhabits my head said,

'Forget about the rope, that's for pussies, just climb down the rock. You can do it.'

Fortunately, a second, wiser and more experienced voice quickly chimed in saying,

'Use the darn rope, idiot. You're not the spring-chicken you used to be.'

I used the rope. Even so, it wasn't easy, and I was relieved to be standing at the base of the cliff a few minutes later. Sadly, the previous year, a seventeen-year-old had lost his footing while climbing Mont Chaudron and fallen twenty metres to his death. I don't know whether this occurred in the same spot, but it seems perfectly plausible.

The hike back to my bike was hot and sweaty as I had to now carry the clothes I'd hidden behind the sign. I had the remains of a bottle of water and two slices of left-over pizza in the bike's top box, so I consumed those while I cooled down a little. The idea of putting my riding gear back on over my sweat soaked clothes wasn't appealing, but I had little choice.

Heading west again towards Larder Lake I noticed that whenever I slowed down, I could hear a faint grinding or scraping which seemed to emanate from the rear wheel. So far, the Suzuki had been relentlessly reliable, starting instantly whether hot or cold and running hiccup-free all day, so to hear unusual noises coming from the rear end was disconcerting to say the least. I'm used to such periodic interruptions of usual service with my old Guzzis. I accept them with forbearance and equanimity as part of the game and am almost disappointed when something doesn't go a little awry. But my super-deluxe modern Suzuki Cavalcade? Surely not!

Wheel bearing? Drive shaft splines? Universal joint? Inevitably one's mind goes straight to the worst-case scenarios. If my U-joint is toast, how am I going to deal with that? Ride the four hundred and fifty miles home and chance it flying apart, wrecking the whole rear end? Call Norm with his trailer? Call CAA?

I rode carefully, not accelerating too hard, trying to pinpoint the noise. Was it there only under power? Was it still there with the clutch pulled in? Only at slow speed or all the time?

In the village of Larder Lake, I pulled over into the parking lane at the side of the road, switched off, put the bike on its centre stand and slid underneath. I spun the rear wheel. Nothing. It sounded completely normal. I grabbed the tire and tried to rock it from side to side, assuming that might tell me if the bearings were shot. Nothing. I carried on, completely mystified, as the rear end continued to chirp cheerfully at me whenever I slowed enough to be able to hear.

A few miles later, in Kirkland Lake, I pulled into yet another Tim's for a break, and, after grabbing my coffee, I wandered back outside and pondered the bike. Could I trust it? Was it going to let me down?

With the bike on the centre stand again, I started it up, put it in gear and gently released the clutch. If I do this on my Guzzis there's usually an almighty clattering as slack in the driveline allows the moving parts to rattle. The Suzuki's rear wheel spun quietly. I increased the revs and the wheel spun faster. No nasty noises. What is this?

By this point I'd convinced myself that there was nothing fundamentally wrong with the bike, and, scraping noises notwithstanding, it was safe to carry on. A few miles later I again slowed, listening for the untoward noises. To my astonishment, all was serene and normal.

I can only assume that while on the gravel parking area back at Mont Chaudron, I'd picked up some gravel dust in the rear disk which had become caught between the disk surface and the pads. Somewhere along the road to Kirkland Lake it must have cleared itself. The back brake was working as well as ever. There were no longer any nasty noises. It was time to boot it for home.

Like any of the big, heavy touring bikes, the Suzuki Cavalcade is an easy bike to ride long and far, but after four hundred and fifty miles and a strenuous hike, by the time I got to Mattawa I was more than ready to stop moving.

I suspect the motel I ended up in had once been more salubrious than it now was. I had a fine view of the Ottawa River, slightly tainted by an evening of overly loud music, broadcast from a work truck, parked next to the river. The shaky wooden staircase leading to my upper-level room was clearly in need of replacement, and the whole place had a 'last gasp' air to it. But the bed was fine, and I slept like a log.

I made another early morning start, reaching home at lunchtime after a few hours and just over two hundred miles. As I'd been riding along, I'd mentally compared the experience of riding the Cavalcade to my old Eldorado as I'd now ridden the same roads and the same distances on both bikes. Despite considerably more power (about twice the HP), more comfortable suspension (ie. it actually has some that functions), a broader and more comfortable seat, and best of all, cruise control, I was riding no further, and was no less tired at the end of the day on the Suzuki as I would have been on the Eldorado. Despite its almost 50-year-old design and the overall sloppiness that comes from time and use, there is something about the way that bike rolls that keeps me happily in the saddle.

But I was just as glad I'd ridden the Suzuki. For this trip, at this time, it turned out to be the ideal bike. Being able to lock my riding gear safely away while I was otherwise engaged was a huge asset, and I found riding the huge beast to be enjoyable – and not at all the uninteresting, appliance-like experience Japanese motorcycles are often accused of. My bottom line, as I'm gradually coming to understand it, is that if the motorbike I'm riding isn't completely dull, the journey is more about the ride than the bike. I'll have to wait and see whether this emerging perspective holds true during my next series of rides.

FIGHTING WITH MY PANTHER[8]

I've been fighting with my Panther ever since I got it. Panther? Not those fierce, desperately cute black leopards that sometimes add a bit of glamour to our television watching – the kind that simultaneously terrify you even though you still want to give them a hug. The Panthers I mean are hard metal.

Back in the Dark Ages of motorcycle history, right at the beginning of the twentieth century, Joah Carver Phelon and Richard Moore entered into partnership producing a range of motorbikes based around a forward sloping, single cylinder engine, where the engine replaced the down-tube of the frame. Sixty years later they were still producing bikes around the same basic architecture. Over the years they had built in many evolutionary changes and modifications leading them to adopt the slogan 'The Perfected Motorcycle' (note the cunning use of 'P' and 'M') – slogan vigorously supported by the international Panther Owners Club whose member frequently refer to 'lesser marques' when describing non-Panther motorbikes.

By the late nineteen sixties, when I first became interested in motorbikes, Panthers had a well-established

---

[8] *First published in 'RealClassic' magazine V.203, March 2021*

reputation as basic, robust, reliable old sloggers – the kind that cloth-capped plumbers and window cleaners might use to drag around a sidecar box full of tools from job to job, and young families from the brick terraces in Bradford and Wolverhampton, could use for their annual trip to the seaside, the kids stuffed into a huge double sidecar.

But times were changing. Cheap cars were starting to be a realistic dream for financially challenged families while old warriors like the Panther M100 and M120, the Norton Big Four and the BSA M21 languished in garden sheds, barely worth the time and effort to try to sell.

For kids like me, lusting after Norton Dominators and BSA Spitfires, these bikes were hardly the stuff of dreams, but they were cheap, available, and generally reliable, as long as you learned the technique to get them started and didn't expect blistering performance.

My own love affair with Panthers started with a 1950 Model M100 Redwing. This was a 600cc single with no rear suspension but with sophisticated Dowty 'Oleomatic' air forks which, despite the abuse I subjected it to, carried me for many happy miles until I abandoned it one rainy day along a Scottish roadside. Shortly after, it was replaced with a 1964 Model M120. This was the 'big one'. 650ccs of thumping single cylinder power which, as legend would have it, fired at every lamppost and could drag a heavy sidecar up the side of a house.

Neither of those legends is remotely true, of course. While it was a relatively slow-revving torquey engine, there were limits to what one could reasonably expect, but it helped me through my college days until the desire to be warmer, drier, and accompanied by girls led me into a world of sluggish and unreliable three-wheelers. But those are stories for another day.

Something about those old bikes stayed with me over

the years. From time to time, I would look at pictures of Panthers on-line and dream of owning one again. Then, out of the blue I encountered a fellow Guzzi enthusiast who also owned a Panther. Time passed, the Panther didn't scratch his itch and eventually it was mine.

Newly acquired 1960 Panther M120 with spares

Initially everything was rosy. Deeply buried in the recesses of my brain I found a memory containing the tricks to reliably starting the bike. These are important tricks as, unless you get it right, Panthers are notorious for backfiring and either launching you over the handlebars or damaging ankles, calves, and tendons. Within a few days of getting the bike home I was happily riding the back roads of my neighbourhood, relishing the delightful boom from the twin silencers and the tractor-like pulses from the big, lazy engine.

At first the revs seemed too high while keeping up with other traffic, but a quick count of the teeth on the engine sprocket told me that the bike was using 'sidecar' gearing. Fortunately, the very active and helpful international Panther Owners Club sold me a new, solo sprocket and in no time the bike was running smoothly and stresslessly on any road. Obviously, it's not a bike for major arterial highways, but can plug along at 55-60 mph quite happily.

For the first thousand miles everything went smoothly. It was comfortable, fun to ride and even the handling and brakes performed acceptably, as long as I remembered I was riding a sixty-year-old bike, designed in the first part of the twentieth century. Then one day it happened. I was on my way home from a lovely 100-mile ride for a pancake lunch, chugging along one of my favourite roads, when I suddenly noticed that the whole outside of the engine was slathered in oil. Up until this point, the Panther had been remarkable oil-tight with only the occasional drip from the primary chaincase to remind me that it was, after all, a British motorcycle of a certain vintage.

I was horrified. Not only was most of the oil on the outside, but it was clear that so much had made its way into the valve cover that instead of keeping the valve stems and rocker arms gently lubricated, the oil was being forced past the exhaust valve, into the combustion chamber and ejected as thick grey smoke through the exhausts.

I checked the oil level. There was still enough in the sump, so I carefully limped home, my right boot shiny with oil dripping from the pushrod tube. Clearly, something had happened to cause excess pressure to build up inside the engine, forcing the oil out through gaskets, seals and O-rings which had hitherto been keeping the oil where it was supposed to be quite successfully. Why the deluge had happened so suddenly and what had caused it was a mystery to me. I had no choice but to start a long, tedious and unsettling process of investigation, analysis and bewilderment.

My grubby little Panther rider's handbook suggested that the oil pump had a rudimentary method of adjusting the flow of oil. It consists of a hole in the oil pump, a ball bearing, a spring and a screwcap to hold the spring in place. Tightening or loosening the screw increases or decreases tension on the spring, either increasing or decreasing the pressure at which oil gets to squeeze past the ball bearing. Cool, thought I. I'll just adjust the screw-thingy and that will cure the problem.

No such luck. No matter what I tried, it didn't make a scrap of difference. As soon as the engine was warm, the oil would start to ooze.

In response to my pitiful requests for help on the Panther Owners Facebook forum, I was told that my flappy valve was almost certainly stuck. "I have a flappy valve?" I thought, wondering whether they were talking about the bike or my heart, and set about finding it. The big nut that holds the drive sprocket onto the end of the crankshaft is usually hidden behind the primary chain case. The nut contains a little disk of metal, about the size of a dime (or a sixpence, for the older UK crowd) which is held loosely in place by a split pin. When the piston is rising, the disk is sucked against a flange so air can't enter the crankcase. When the piston descends, the disk is pushed off the flange allowing crankcase pressure to escape. The idea is that if the air can escape, crankcase pressure will be relieved, and the oil won't be forced out of every seal and orifice like mine.

So, I investigated the flappy valve. I cleaned it. I checked it. I even took the nut off and sucked and blew just to make sure it was working properly (it was). I put it all back together and………like an oil tanker stranded on the rocks – oil everywhere again. It was time to go in for a coffee and a think.

That think lasted quite a while. I had other bikes to ride and places to go. Weeks passed before I was back out in the garage pondering the Panther. While idly investigating potential sources of the problem I kept myself busy by making sure all the exterior nuts and bolts were fully tightened. The Panther's cylinder head is attached to the rest of the bike by four long bolts which thread into the crankcase and two smaller ones which protrude between the fins at the front and rear of the engine. I gave them all a tweak. The ones on the right side and at the front and rear snugged up nicely, but as I tightened those on the left side, I could tell that the steel studs were working their way out of the aluminium case. Arghhh. That is not what I wanted.

A few miles from where I live resides a man with special machining skills. Could he put some new, threaded inserts into the crankcase? He could? Cool. So, I stripped the engine, removed it from the frame, carted it over in the back of my car and more-or-less forgot about it over the winter.

Eventually spring arrived and with-it thoughts of chuffing along pleasant back roads on the Panther, so retrieving the engine, I hurried home and started the time consuming, but admittedly simple process of putting it all back together.

Engine out, heading for repair (before the Guzzi gearbox - that's another story)

This is going to sound too good to be true, because old, single cylinder bikes can be difficult to start, especially when they've just been in pieces, but on the very first kick, the bike roared into life and, after a couple of minutes, settled into a nice steady idle. I let it sit, chugging away quietly while I listened for the asthmatic wheezing through the flappy valve.

At first all was well. Even as the engine warmed up there were no signs of oil leaks, but as soon as I had ridden a couple of miles, the top of the engine case was awash in oil dripping steadily from the pushrod tunnel. I'm not usually given to flinging tools across the garage or other external signs of annoyance and disappointment, but I must admit, a few choice words might have been heard, had anyone been within earshot.

Once again, I queried the knowledgeable folks on the Panther forum and combed the internet for any clues to explain the excess crankcase pressure that was clearly at the root of the problem.

'There must be too much blow-by past the piston rings' wise and experienced Panther gurus advised me. I knew that the piston and rings were new and had been fitted to the cylinder before I got the bike. It had travelled less than a hundred miles before I got my hands on it and still only had just over a thousand. Oh well, I'd better have a look.

I pulled off the fuel tank, loosened the head-steady, removed the valve gear, unbolted the cylinder head, and, with a little jiggling and loosening of engine bolts managed to slide the barrel off the piston.

Hmm. That's curious! I could see the tiniest scoring on the cylinder walls and piston skirt, but more worryingly, the piston wasn't moving freely on the gudgeon pin. Why on earth folks in the UK call it a gudgeon pin is beyond me. A gudgeon is a small freshwater fish which looks nothing like the tube of shiny metal that holds the piston to the connecting rod. In other parts of the world, it's called a wrist pin – a far more informative, if more boring descriptor.

Weird terminology notwithstanding, my gudgeon wasn't doing its job. The piston should have been able to flop smoothly on the end of the con rod. Mine would move but it was stiff. Instead of sliding smoothly up and down the cylinder, perhaps the stiffness was causing the piston to angle slightly in the bore, allowing gasses to escape past the rings and into the crankcase. Although all the engine internals were new, I decided to bite the metaphorical bullet and get a new piston with the cylinder rebored or honed to fit.

Once he'd had a good look at my parts, Karl, at the local machine shop, declared that the old piston was from a Harley Shovelhead – and replacements were readily available – the only question remaining being whether I wanted to go with the cheaper cast version, or lay out the big bucks for a Wiseco forged piston.

Under normal circumstances I would probably have opted for the cheapest alternative, but I'd just been reading Des Molloy's inspirational books *'The Last Hurrah'* (from China to Holland) and *'No One Said it Would be Easy'* (in South America) about his monumental travels on his aged Panther 'Penelope', and I was full of ambition to ride my own Panther to exotic and distant parts.

'Let's go with the Wiseco, Karl' I said, gulping slightly as I thought of the extra $100 that would add to the bill, while desperately hoping that I'd need to worry less about major engine troubles down the line.

Eventually the piston arrived, the barrel was cleaned up to suit and I was ready to put the bike back together. I diligently massaged the gudgeon pin and its mating surfaces until the piston moved smoothly and easily, slid the barrel over the piston rings, jiggled the cylinder head into position, then bolted everything back in place. Once again it was time to hear it run.

I'd noticed that the new piston had a slightly higher crown than the one it was replacing. It still fit nicely in the combustion chamber with plenty of clearance for the valves, but I soon found out that it had also noticeably raised the compression. I'm no lightweight but I could now stand with my full weight on the kickstart with it at ninety degrees – and it wouldn't budge.

The time-tested way to start these big singles is to pull in the decompression lever, which opens the exhaust valve slightly, ease the piston past top-dead-centre, then, with the ignition on, give a mighty kick. Once again, the bike obliged by starting immediately. Once again, it idled nicely until well warmed up. And once again, oil started working its way past seals and O-rings as soon as the bike had done a couple of miles. Darn it! What on earth was I missing?

Months passed. Either I was hiding inside avoiding those nasty, spiky, alien Covid bugs, or I was out on one of the other bikes enjoying one of the few activities one could engage in with little likelihood of infection. The Panther languished in the corner of the garage until the wet autumn weather started to impede my riding and I'd gradually built up enough enthusiasm to take another crack at it.

Sometimes our minds build relatively simple tasks to monstrous proportions. Taking the Panther to pieces for another look was such a task. In reality, it's an easy, straightforward motorcycle to disassemble. Tank off (I hadn't even fully bolted it on since last time), carb off, remove the whacking big castings that hold the top of the engine to the frame, and unscrew and drop the exhaust pipes. Unbolt the valve cover, taking care not to damage the gasket I'd so carefully manufactured out of gasket paper last time around, and remove the rocker arms and pushrods. Unbolt the four big engine bolts and the two smaller ones under the head, and pull the head off. It takes a little jiggling to remove the cylinder head but eventually that heavy cast iron lump is lying on the floor. Gently rotate the engine until the piston is at the bottom of its stroke and slide the barrel off. Man, it weighs a ton. Stick a rag in the top of the engine case to stop the con-rod flopping around, and we're done. Nothing to it. Why had I turned it into such a major event? It probably took me less than two hours.

With the engine partially disassembled I started looking for troubles. The most obvious source of crankcase pressure would be if air was squeezing past the piston rings. This would leave dirty smears on the cylinder wall – but no, the walls were squeaky clean. What else could it be?

The rear of the cylinder has a little oil-feed channel that

squirts oil through a tiny hole in the cylinder wall below the piston skirt. I found there were three tiny holes, two of which had been blocked off. Could this be the source of the problem? I measured the height of the lowest hole and compared it with the up and down movement of the piston, but it seemed to be in the right place. Perhaps too much oil was getting through. I decided to block the hole, figuring that the thrashing flywheels would be throwing up more than enough oil mist to keep the cylinder wall properly lubricated.

During one of my many re-assemblies I'd noticed a slight bubbling at the cylinder head gasket. This is a thin copper ring. I'd read somewhere that if they have been in use for a while, they tend to get stiff and don't seal well, so I annealed it by throwing it on the kitchen stove, turning up the heat until it was nice and red. Yes, my wife was out...

Everything else seemed to be working properly. The piston moved smoothly and evenly in the barrel, so I put the engine back together, kicked it into life and went for a short ride.

Bad idea! I was less than a mile from my house when I felt the bike slowing. I instantly pulled in the clutch, cut the engine, and pulled to the side of the road. After giving it a moment to cool and with the ignition off and the valve lifter open, I tried the kickstart. The piston slid up and down the cylinder with no nasty noises, so I went through my usual starting routine, turned on the ignition and gave her a spin. Once again, the Panther started and sat happily ticking over while I put on my gloves.

Getting home was going to be a trick. There's a long, steep hill between where I was and where I was heading, so I took it easy, stayed in the lower gears to avoid any lugging and gingerly headed up the hill, my fingers hovering over the clutch lever. The instant I felt the engine balking I squeezed the clutch and let the engine die. This could turn out to be the longest mile for quite a while.

Another few minutes passed. She started up again with no untoward noises and I was able to crest the hill and coast home without any further trouble. Clearly, thinking I knew more than generations of Phelon and Moore engineers was a delusion. It was time, once again, to strip the engine and open up that oil-way. Oh well, we live and learn.

1960 Panther M120

Saturday morning arrived and with it the time and enthusiasm to get to grips once again with my truculent friend. By now I was a practiced hand at taking the Panther to pieces. In less than two hours I had the cylinder head off and the barrel loose on the main engine studs. This time I didn't remove the barrel – I rotated the engine until the piston was at the top of its travel. This gave me enough space to unblock the oil channel I'd so stupidly blocked off without sliding the barrel off the piston or disturbing the piston rings. With the outer primary chain case off I scrupulously cleaned and reset the 'flappy' valve that vents the crankcase. Then, making sure the little hole in the base gasket lined up with the oil channel, I stitched the whole thing back together.

After a quick lunch I wheeled the bike outside, gave it a kick and to my enormous relief and pleasure, it fired up immediately. No nasty noises, and once it warmed up a bit, a nice steady tick-over and all the right mechanical sounds. The flappy valve was doing its thing – puffing air out as the piston descended and sealing up tight as the piston rose. Time to go for a spin.

I quickly replaced the left side footrest but left the primary chain case cover off so I could check the puffing action of the flappy valve and enjoy the risk of grinding my heel on the rotating clutch nuts. My short test circuit takes me through my little rural subdivision, down a hill towards Collins Lake, along the lakeshore road for about a mile, then back up the valley edge on a little unpaved track through the woods. It's just long enough to get the bike properly warmed up and has enough variety that all the gears get used at various revs. A beaver had caused a small washout at one of the culverts, so I had to navigate a foot-deep gully across the track. I stopped momentarily to think about it, but deciding it was well within the Panther's capabilities I plugged on.

Back at home in my driveway I was thrilled to find no nasty signs of excessive leakage, a flappy valve that was cheerfully chuffing air from the crankcase and an engine that felt ready for some real road miles. And then it snowed! Oh well. The winter will give me a chance to tidy things up a bit and you never know, once it gets cold and sunny so the roads become dry, I may be able to sneak out for some longer exploratory rides.

Postscript: Spring arrived, and I was able to take the Panther for a few short rides. After ten or fifteen miles, she still oozed a little oil, but it was down to a manageable drooling, not the unsettling, engine-drenching mess it once was. I've been systematically cleaning up every source as they appear. It's usually something simple – an oil line that doesn't quite seal, or an engine case nut that has vibrated loose. Each time I go out, the leaks are less, and the bike runs just a little better.

Either I'm getting used to her, or she's getting used to me. I've managed some two-hundred-mile days without any significant leaks or catastrophes. I think we've finally reached détente.

MISSINAIBI RIVER

There are disadvantages to being an eternal optimist. Before I set out for northern Ontario, I'd had a quick look at the weather ap on my phone. 'No rain for 59 minutes' for our local area, it said, so I quickly checked for Perth which was on my route. The prognosis looked good. I jumped on the Suzuki Cavalcade and headed north. A wise person might have paid a little more attention to the details, and perhaps looked a tad more attentively at the overall forecast, but always assuming the best, I hit the road.

By the time I reached Westport twenty miles later, the skies were darkening, and as I rode the winding highway along the Mississippi River between Playfairville and Lanark, the road surface was awash with rain. Lovely road it is, but the local maintenance crews have absolutely plastered it with 'tar snakes' – those shiny, black linear crack repairs which are the bane of motorcyclists – and they had become treacherous in the rain. I had been debating whether to stop and put on my rain gear, reluctant to add the bulky clothing over my already bulky riding gear. I was glad I did. By the time I reached Lanark, it was raining so hard that I could no longer safely ride, so I pulled over and watched as torrents flowed down the gutters and thunder rumbled in the sky.

Eventually the storm slowed and it was safe enough for me to resume riding. I could feel that a little damp had seeped in around my buttocks, but other than that, the rain gear had done its job and I was still basically dry.

I had got it into my head to visit the Missinaibi River Provincial Park. Forty-two years ago, Chris (my wife) and I had been doing some archaeological survey work on some nearby lakes and visited the park briefly. In my memory, the road in from Chapleau was a long, bumpy gravel and dust thread through the forest, and I wondered if, and how much it had changed. But first I had to get there.

I had been chatting with a friend near Renfrew who was in the process of rebuilding an old Moto Guzzi 850T. He had taken a fancy to the lines of an old seat that, once upon a time had graced my Guzzi 750s. The seat is a complete disaster – the metal seat pan has completely rotted away; the foam has deteriorated and the leather covering is torn and rotting. Still, he was sure he could use it as a template, and since his house was on the way I'd promised to drop it off.

My altruism was tempered by self-interest. He and his wife have dogs, lots of them – mostly German Shepherds – and I needed a dog fix. After having a series of German Shepherds myself over the last thirty years, I miss not having a dog and ache to get my hands in their fur. Fortunately, when I arrived at Avalon Ranch I was greeted by a beautiful young female who decided that my face was in serious need of a good licking. And yes, I'm still talking about dogs.

Damp, cool, periods of rain. That just about describes my long haul north through La Vérendrye Park to Val d'Or, then west through Rouyn-Noranda and back into Ontario. My original plan had been to camp in Esker Lakes Provincial Park, a mere twelve miles north of the highway, but another thorough soaking during a thunderstorm as I navigated through the industrial heart of Rouyn-Noranda, convinced me otherwise. I'd been intending to have a warm-up coffee at the Tim Hortons in Kirkland Lake, but when I saw the Super 8 motel next door the ride was over.

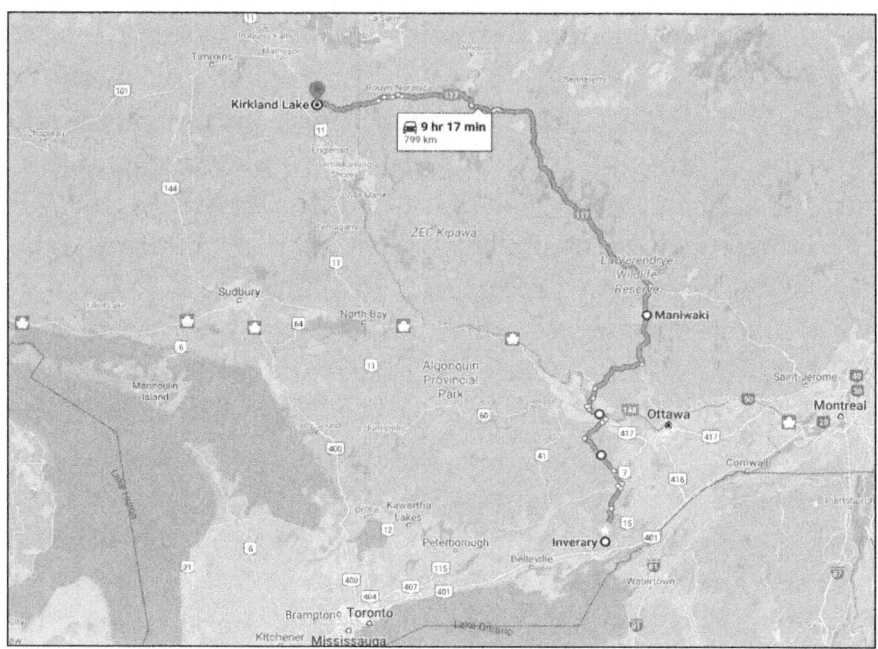

After putting an egregious amount on my credit card and some faffing around with plastic room keys that wouldn't work, I finally settled into my warm but undistinguished room and called it a day. Google maps tells me I'd ridden 496 miles and it felt like it. No complaints about the bike though. Rain, wind, and distance seemed to have no effect on it. It had soldiered on in its calm, imperturbable manner, doing everything I asked of it smoothly and well, as long as I kept pouring combustible liquids down its throat. It can be forgiven for being a thirsty beast. It's no lightweight.

Morning arrived cool and damp — about like my mood. I'm usually a fairly buoyant person but sometimes, for no obvious reason, my normal enthusiasm shrivels, and I feel a bit flat. A large coffee and muffin from the Tim Horton's next door helped a little but by the time I had repacked the bike and swung back out onto the highway, I was just going through the motions.

The scenery wasn't helping. On a grey day the route between Kirkland Lake and Timmins isn't very inspiring. Even on the sunniest of days it's hardly likely to get one's aesthetic juices flowing. The landscape is flat and treed, punctuated by a few scabby houses and the occasional field, and once past Matheson, Highway 101 is dead straight for thirty miles, then only very slightly curvy until you hit South Porcupine and the edges of the built-up area.

Timmins and South Porcupine are gold mining towns, and it shows in the vast fenced areas, mining buildings and the ruined landscapes that surround them. Gold bearing rocks had been discovered at the turn of the twentieth century, leading to the 'Porcupine Gold Rush' of 1909. Gold is still mined in the area and is the driving force which keeps the towns alive.

It's amazing how little things can easily lighten one's mood. In this case two little things. As I approached the edge of town a large male black bear was happily grazing in a meadow immediately adjacent to one of the fenced-off mining areas. I did a quick mirror-check, spun around and rode back grabbing my camera from the handy recess in the Cavalcade's faux tank. The bear looked up, then, determining that I wasn't any kind of threat, went back to eating whatever he had found. Black bears are omnivorous – basically everything is food. He may have found some roadkill and dragged it into the field for a peaceful nosh, but it was just as likely that he was grazing on grass like a short, black, muscle-bound cow. I left him to it, spun the bike around again, and headed into town.

Few people will head to northern Ontario looking for

architectural gems, and if they were deluded enough to try, they would be deeply disappointed. The buildings lining the main road into Timmins are strictly functional, square, low, blocky things, built to enclose space, with no thought given to pleasing the eye, so I was shocked to have my attention rivetted by the Chamber of Commerce building at the first major intersection. Some brilliantly imaginative person had painted a perfectly ordinary grey office building with a massive and stunningly beautiful multi-coloured raven clutching a piece of rock in its talons. It is a dazzling piece of work which brightened my whole day.

Despite the light rain and drizzle that persisted during the next hour or two of riding, I had become surprisingly content. The road continued to be a thin ribbon of tarmac through endless trees, and even though the clouds were grey and gloomy, I'd begun to enjoy myself again. Occasionally there would be a break in the trees as I passed a lake, creek or wetland, or the road would rise over a low hill with areas of exposed bedrock beside the road. I set the cruise control in the general vicinity of the posted speed limit, sat back and relaxed.

From time to time I'd be conscious of a twinge developing in my right hip. I don't know if it is the beginnings of arthritis or my body just complaining because the joint has been sitting in the same position for hours. I put my feet on the crash bars. I shuffled them back and forwards on the pegs. Sometimes I'd hang a leg to trail my foot along the road surface. Occasionally I'd even stand up – anything to change position for a few minutes to relieve the pressure. Then, mysteriously, the pain would go away and I'd find I'd been riding for another hour without giving it a thought.

Foleyet lies roughly half way between Timmins and Chapleau. I pulled off the highway to fill up at the surprisingly pleasant and comprehensively stocked general store, the sign board for which announces: *'If we don't have it, you don't need it!'*. Although Foleyet isn't ever going to draw people to it for its beauty, it is a vital node on the highway. My fuel had been getting low, and without the gas station, I would almost certainly have had to use up my five litre 'emergency' supply which I had strapped to the passenger footboard. A quick spin around the town (pop. 193) revealed the railway yard, a few dismal wooden houses, some of which appeared to be vacant, a restaurant and the LCBO liquor store. The restaurant was closed – possibly a Covid victim – but, predictably, the LCBO was still in business.

Pulling back onto the highway for another hour of gentle droning to Chapleau, my mind was racing ahead to the fifty miles of gravel road between Chapleau and the Missinaibi River Provincial Park. Was this a stupid idea? Would I be able to control almost half a ton of bike, rider and gear on loose and soft surfaces on street tires? What if I drop it? What if it drops on me? In the end I decided that since the sky wasn't falling and it is just another road, with a bit of care and attention I should be fine.

I always prefer to start off with a full tank, so although I'd only just filled up, I topped off the tank, grabbed a coffee and apple fritter at the gas station on the outskirts of

Chapleau and headed into town looking for any signs that would point me in the right direction.

Circumnavigating the oddly convoluted railway overpass, I was just about to worry that I'd already missed my turn when I saw a sign pointing to 'Chapleau Game Reserve'. 'That must be the way' I thought, and I was right, although not for the right reasons. The Chapleau Game Preserve is a vast, 2700 square mile (roughly 2 million acres) tract of land north of Chapleau with Missinaibi Lake roughly at its centre. Reputedly the largest game preserve in the world, it was established in 1925 as a protected area in response to over hunting and trapping once the Canadian Pacific and Canadian National Railways brought easy access to the area. I should have been looking for signs to the provincial park, but if there were any as I left Chapleau, I missed them.

The outskirts of towns like Chapleau are almost always the same. There are a few scrubby industrial buildings, plenty of abandoned machinery, piles of gravel and wood and some scattered down-at-heel houses. So far, the gravel road was wide and well-traveled and I found myself thinking, 'well, if it's all like this – no problem'. Once past the weigh-scale the road bifurcated. With no signs to tell me otherwise, I followed the most heavily travelled route, almost immediately ending up in a timber storage yard for one of the logging companies.

The first person I asked for directions was busy cleaning dog poo off the otherwise spotless fabric seats of his new work truck. His little companion had had an explosive accident. He too was a stranger to the area, so I left him to his unpleasant task and wandered over to where another guy was adjusting the load straps on his tandem-trailer log truck.

He quickly informed me that I'd missed the turn,

pointed me in the right direction, and cautioned me to be careful, as his company was actively hauling along the route. That meant I could expect to encounter fully loaded logging trucks, traveling at high speed, taking up most of the road. Oh joy!

Many of the roads that reach north into the forest are private, constructed and maintained by the logging companies. Other travelers, such as myself, are tolerated, but the trucks have, and take right-of-way, and it would be a foolish rider who tried to dispute it. It's not that the drivers are madmen, but these are huge vehicles, travelling long distances over rough surfaces with heavy loads. Once moving, they're not eager to stop, and since they rarely encounter other traffic, they take up most of the road, tending to swing wide on the corners, spraying gravel and dust in all directions. The last thing they expect to see is some clown on a motorbike, weaving around in the loose gravel as they romp around a bend.

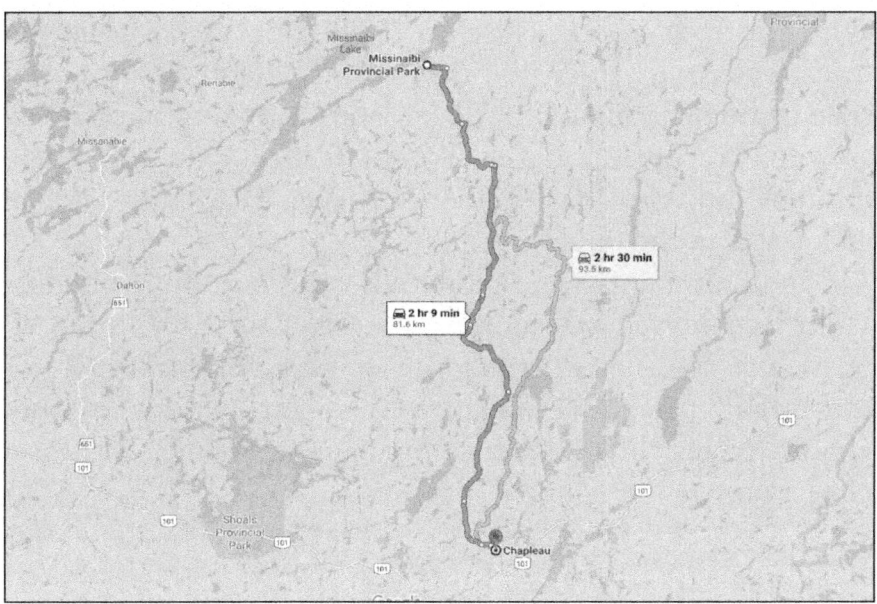

So I made sure I stayed vigilant. Near the bends, I stayed close to the side of the road, preferring to fight it out in the loose gravel than chance encountering countless tons of logging truck barreling my way. It's not always easy to keep an eye on your mirrors when you're trying to make sure the front wheel isn't heading for disaster, but a quick check now and then usually told me there was nothing behind – until there was.

Most of the time I was chugging along in third gear, the tach hovering around 2000 rpm and my road speed staying well below 40. Occasionally, when the road surface was particularly good I might snick it into fourth for a few moments, but it never lasted long before I was back into third, or even second gear. But with an empty logging truck closing in fast from behind, I changed to second, moved over into the loose gravel, and focused on remaining loose as the handlebars danced in my hands and the front wheel fought for traction. I was almost at stall speed. Not for the first time was I glad of the Cavalcade's considerable torque. With the tach diving close to 1000 rpm, as soon as the truck was past I open the throttle and gradually increased speed, moving out of the loose and onto the hardpacked surface. I chewed on the cloud of road dust for a few minutes, but that was far better than a face in the gravel and a bike in the ditch.

Such moments were mercifully rare, but after this one, I did find myself questioning the logic of riding such an unsuitable bike where conditions could be unsettling, if not downright dangerous. Then the bike hit some soft sand, almost jerking the bars out of my hands. Whew! That was a close one.

Why do I do this? Why seek out long gravel roads heading generally north? After careful thought – and, over the years I've had plenty of time to consider this – I have decided it is because riding on these roads requires total concentration. There's never a moment when you can let your thoughts wander. You have to be 'on' the whole time. You just can't let the Lizard Brain handle the bike - every fragment of your grey matter has to be engaged. And because one's mind is so tightly focused, time passes incredibly quickly.

We all know that time isn't a constant. Einstein used mathematics to show that, and sometimes we experience it ourselves. I regularly set out along some lonely road, assuming the ride will take hours, only to arrive at my destination far ahead of my expectations. I suppose I could argue that the level of concentration required to stay upright makes time seem to pass more quickly – but I prefer to believe that there's some weird physics at work. Perhaps, if Einstein were still around, we could encourage him to do some back-country riding and see what he thinks.

With time romping along, I was soon beyond the active haul road. The last twenty miles into the park were along a much narrower road with a single set of tire tracks down the middle. It was still just wide enough for two vehicles to pass without clipping wing mirrors, but it was clear that everyone stuck to the middle unless forced to do otherwise. I planted the Cavalcade's wheels in the nearside track and carried on. The ground was well-packed and a delight to ride on.

I stopped to catch my breath at a small timber bridge, relishing the total absence of any human noise other than the gentle ticking of the Suzuki's cooling engine. When I set off again, almost immediately, a medium-sized Black Bear crossed the road ahead. I'd noticed some piles of bear poo along the road as I'd been riding, but it's always a pleasure to see the animals in the flesh, even if you rarely get more than a glimpse of a large black shape diving back into the cover of the forest. Bears like to use the roads as their highways, and who can blame them? If you have somewhere to go, it's far easier to use the road than struggle through the dense forest. And there are lots of them. According to a provincial government web site, the Chapleau Game Preserve has the highest density of Black Bears in Ontario. Not to worry though. They were not likely to launch themselves out of the bush at me, preferring to scuttle off at the first sign or sound of humans.

In what seemed like no time at all, I'd passed the sign at the edge of the park, ridden the last four miles to the gatehouse and wandered in to see if they had camping space for me. A sensible person might have booked ahead before setting off down fifty miles of bush road, but I didn't, figuring that if they were full, with countless thousands of square miles of bush around, I'd find somewhere to put my tiny tent.

As it turned out, I needn't have worried. Other than a handful of fishermen's RVs near the boat dock, I had the place to myself. The uniformed warden at the gatehouse took my money, and in response to my request for somewhere quiet, allocated me site 16, well away from the RVs and conveniently close to the little path leading to the beach. My little one-person tent was dwarfed by the space available, so I tucked it discretely close to the edge of the forest and wandered off to explore, heading straight for the lake.

Missinaibi Lake is a monster. Shaped like a tuning fork, its main arm is thirty miles long and even the northwest arm is twelve miles long. To put it in perspective, with a surface area of over 19,000 acres, it is almost five times as large as England's largest lake, Lake Windermere. From my position on the shore, I could only see a tiny fraction. I sat for a while, listening to little waves rippling along the shore before making my way across quartz-veined rocks around a headland. It was very peaceful.

Sometimes I get carried away talking about places where there is no sound or sign of human activity, and given my frequent references to enjoying being alone, one might assume I'm a misanthropist. Not true. Although I think humanity has become a plague on this planet and will soon make it uninhabitable for our species, I actually like people quite a lot. We are fascinating, creative, remarkable, funny, vicious, vindictive little monkeys, capable of amazing, wonderful and sometimes ghastly things. Enjoying one's own company and finding pleasure in places where other people are not, and relishing the society of others, are not mutually exclusive.

Missinaibi Lake

I spent the rest of the evening exploring the various paths around the campsite before filling my stomach with a supper of raisins, apple sauce, cheese and a couple of granola bars. Being moderately bear-wise, I ate at the picnic table, locked the remaining food in the Cavalcade's top box and didn't bring so much as a crumb of anything edible into the tent when I retired. It was not, perhaps, the most comfortable night I've ever spent, as my thin camper mat had developed a leak, but I slept, untroubled by thoughts of marauding bears or hostile primates.

I must admit, as I set off next morning, a miniscule, insecure part of me was thinking, 'I got away with riding this lumbering beast on that road yesterday, I wonder if I'll be so lucky today?' But in the end, by taking it easy, always planning where my front wheel was going next, and keeping my death-grip on the handlebars to a dull roar, I was soon riding along enjoying myself. Within moments of leaving the park boundary another Black Bear crossed ahead of me – one of the three I'd see that morning. Actually, that's not strictly true. I saw two. I only became conscious of the third when it was pointed out by one of my Youtube viewers, that a moving black shape was visible on one of my videos as I re-crossed the wooden bridge. This is the second time my camera has caught bears I hadn't noticed while I was riding. It makes me wonder how often I miss them (and other creatures) while I'm concentrating on the road ahead.

Back in Chapleau I refueled again then headed south down Highway 129 – the Chapleau Highway. This isn't exactly a busy road. Somewhere between 300 and 400 vehicles pass along it each day and it's often possible to ride for long periods without seeing any other traffic.

It was raining again. The logging truck ahead of me was throwing up a fine mist so I dropped well back, content to burble along with the engine barely working. Eventually we both had to slow for some roadworks and the driver encouraged me to pass him. Perhaps he was fed up with me trailing him, but, more likely, he was a rider too, and knew what pleasures lay ahead, as we were just about to enter the most delightful part of the route, where the road follows every twist and turn of the broad, shallow Mississagi River for many miles.

Where the road closely follows the river, there are no safety barriers. Lose concentration for a moment and you would find yourself careening down a steep bank into the cool, clear water. Even though the road surface is generally good and the curves entrancing, to ride this road fast would be miss the point entirely. It is a road for dawdling, for enjoying the scenery, for watching the river and for scanning the high valley cliffs for wildlife.

The truck was now far behind and with nothing ahead, I pulled the Cavalcade over to the narrow band of gravel between the road and the river and took some pictures. The rear tire had sunk in a few inches, and when I pulled away, the wheel spun as it sought for grip in the loose rocks and sand. Torque is a wonderful thing. In mere moments the bike had pulled itself back on to the road and we were heading south.

Just beyond Tunnel Lake Highway 129 veers southwest towards Thessalon while I opted to take the short-cut across to Iron Bridge, saving a few miles of droning on the Trans-Canada Highway. The short-cut traverses a belt of quiet, rolling, pastoral land sandwiched between the shores of Lake Huron and the Canadian Shield uplands to the north. It is a world of scattered farms, meadows and hay fields on the rich clay soils deposited in the bed of the ancient glacial Lake Algonquin. After the endless forests further north, it was enjoyable to be able to look out across the fields, trying to pick out fragments of the old lake shore, now visible as rounded ridges across the landscape.

Once again, the Cavalcade had chewed its way through most of a tank of fuel so I stopped at the first gas station in Iron Bridge. If I'm easy on the throttle I can just about squeeze 190 miles from its 23 litre tank, but with fuel stops few and far between, I prefer to top up whenever the opportunity presents itself. I would have to refuel three more times before I opened my garage door but the Cavalcade's thirst is a small price to pay to be able to waft along in such comfort. With many hours of riding to go, I found David Sedaris's audiobook *'When you are engulfed in flames'* on my phone, connected to my Bluetooth headset, and hit the road again.

The first few hours were a monotonous haul along the Trans-Canada Highway, then south, heading in the direction of Toronto. My GPS was telling me that the quickest route was to head straight for Toronto, then veer left along the incredibly tedious multi-lane Highway 401 – the main highway between Windsor/Detroit and Montreal. But speed and efficiency aren't everything. I opted to turn left just beyond Parry Sound to follow a series of secondary highways east through the heart of the best parts of eastern Ontario. It was certainly not the fastest way home, but the curvy roads, the minimal traffic and the constant company of rocks, lakes and trees made for an enjoyable ride.

As the warm afternoon cooled into evening, I stopped beside Denbigh Lake to pull on some warmer clothes before settling in for the last two hours on the road. By the time I pulled into my driveway it was 10pm. Other than brief stops for fuel and to swallow a few mouthfuls of raisins, I had been riding solidly for sixteen hours.

Three long days in the saddle, a hundred miles of high-intensity gravel riding in and out of the park, a night under nylon with the sound of the lake lulling me to sleep, a handful of bears, and a long, exhausting ride through pleasant country on the way home. Now that's my kind of ride.

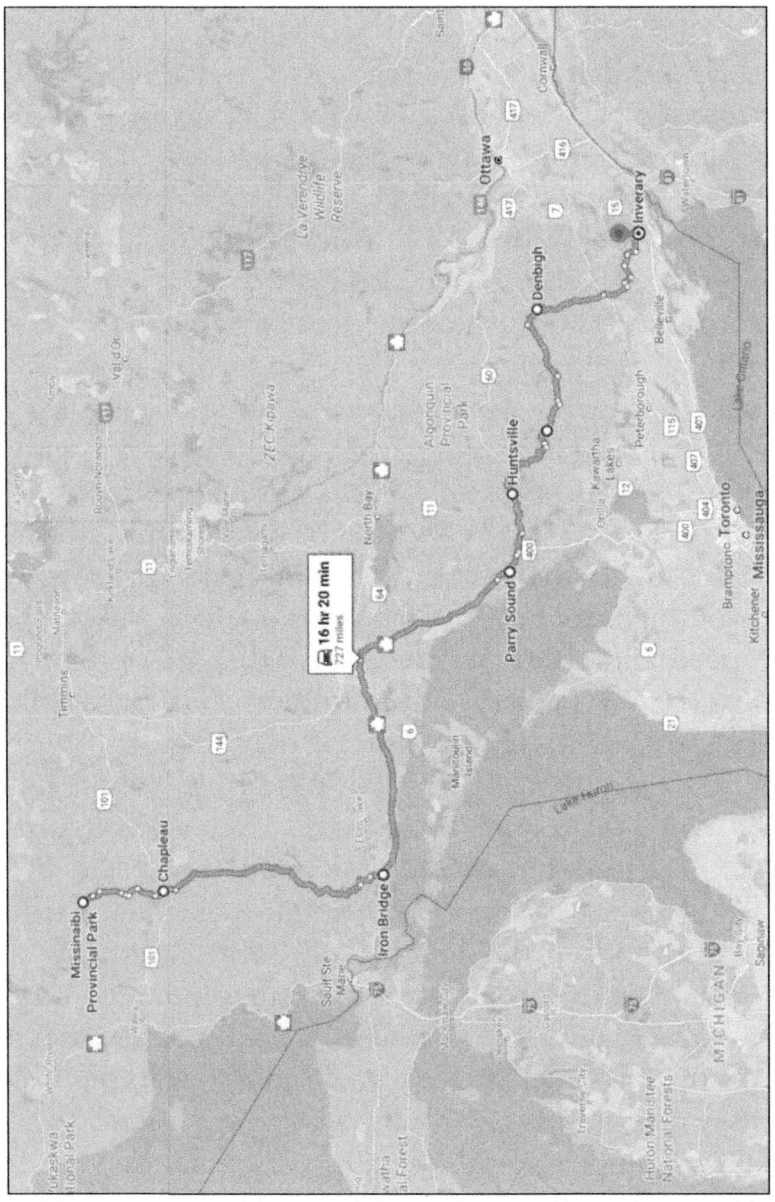

MISSISSAGI

I sleep naked. It was a warm night and I wasn't even covered by my sleeping bag when the crash of my heavy tool bag falling to the ground not twenty feet away awoke me. Something large and strong was messing with my bike – and it wasn't a human.

I had ridden the Eldorado the four hundred and seventy five miles from home to Mississagi Provincial Park that day. It had been a long, uneventful ride but after a five-thirty start and eleven hours in the saddle, I was tired and fell asleep before it was fully dark. My tiny, one-person tent was in a small clearing in the forest, just back from the lake shore. Other campers in RVs were discretely parked on their own sites – the closest about fifty metres away and well screened by trees. I was probably snoring merrily.

Before lying down I had closed the panniers, set my phone to charge inside my tank bag and placed the bag containing my few scraps of food – some peanuts, some leftover crisps and some biscuits – on the seat, weighed down by my tool bag. I should have hung it from a tree. I know better than to leave food accessible in bear country.

Suddenly wide awake, I could hear the sound of something large and noisy over at the bike. My flashlight was in the tank bag. My knife – as if a knife would have done anything other than provide me with an opportunity to cut myself – was sitting on my desk at home. I had no way to see what was going on and no way to protect myself. Naked in the dark, I felt uniquely vulnerable.

It took me ages to find the tent zipper while outside, the sound of snuffling, scuffling, dragging and grunting made me wonder what was happening to my poor bike. Eventually I got the zipper open and leaned my head outside. I could see absolutely nothing. I couldn't even see the bike, let alone whatever it was that was making all the noise. I shouted 'Oi', then ducked back inside.

Deep inside, we know we are just weak, scared little monkeys, and no match for the predatory beasts that inhabit our nightmares. If a predator had decided that it wanted to tear my bike apart, who was I to argue? I certainly wasn't about to clamber out of the tent, stark naked, to confront whatever it was. I zipped the tent and lay, listening to the grumbling, bumping and scraping going on not twenty feet from my head.

Surprisingly, I was unexpectedly calm. The creature had clearly found what it was interested in and was unlikely to come to investigate the anxious human in the nearby tent. So I lay, listening, until the sounds of dragging and grumbling gradually moved away into the forest and quiet descended again. No matter what had happened, there was nothing I could do until daylight. I pulled my sleeping bag over me and was soon asleep.

I awoke to half-light and the rumbling sounds of an approaching thunderstorm. My toolbag was lying beside the bike where it had fallen, the tank bag and panniers were untouched, but the ripstop nylon bag section containing my food was gone. I looked around expecting to find its shredded remains, but it was nowhere in sight. As the storm broke, I scuttled back to my tent and lay, listening to the booming and crackling in the sky and the drumming of the rain on the flysheet.

Eventually the storm fizzled out and I was able to

dress, retrieve my rain suit from the bike and head into the forest to search for my missing pack. Pushing through rain soaked cedar and spruce in ever widening circles, I began to wonder whether I would ever find it, and was just about to abandon the search when there it was, lying in a hollow near the base of a large tree. To my astonishment, other than a rip in the transparent map cover and a few small tooth marks it was undamaged – and even more surprising, the contents were untouched.

The nighttime sounds, the casual throwing off of my heavy tool bag, the grumbling and dragging had convinced me that I was being raided by a large animal. I was sure it was a bear. But the toothmarks, and the animal's inability to rip the bag apart told a different story. This was no bear. A bear would have torn into that bag as if it were paper. My food bag must have been stolen by a rascally raccoon.

At night, in the dark, sounds are amplified and our minds always construct the worst case scenario. But even if I'd had a flashlight, a knife and some clothes on, I wouldn't have been arguing with a raccoon. Those guys are feisty!

The thunderstorm had cleared the skies, bringing fresh, cool air scented with wet pine and cedar. Most of the other campers had yet to stir, so I rolled out of the campsite as quietly as the booming exhausts on my bike would allow, and was soon heading north towards the Little White River Road. This is one of my favourites and for good reason. For most of its forty miles it hugs the bank of the Little White River which romps along in an almost unbroken series of rapids and riffles as it twists and turns through forested hills. It is deeply lovely. It's a road to be relished at low speed, partly because the road surface is usually a bit rough, but partly because racing along would be to simply miss the point.

As I approached the central part of the road, the rough pavement gave way to rough gravel, and it wasn't long before I passed a road roller and shortly thereafter, a couple of road crew workers. The roller was the first vehicle I'd seen that morning.

At about the mid-point, the road crosses the river so that, instead of having the river to your left, it is now to the right, but as before, the road hugs the riverbank, twisting and turning with every bend, until it spits you out into open farming country for the last few miles to Iron Bridge.

Why was I here at all? Well, it's odd how things work out. Back at home I'd been thinking of another short trip to northern Ontario but hadn't a firm focus or destination in mind, when someone on the ADV internet forum mentioned Dunn's Valley – a tiny hamlet in the rolling back-country north of Bruce Mines. Decades ago, when I first arrived in Canada, I'd been living in an apartment in Sault Ste. Marie but decided that I didn't leave crowded Britain to live in a Canadian city, so I'd rented an old farm house near Dunn's Valley. I needed to experience the 'Canadian wilds' and the farm house certainly fulfilled that requirement. It lay on its own, in a small patch of meadow, at the end of a narrow road, surrounded by forested hills. It was a hour's drive to my work in the Soo . It was about as remote as you could get.

I'd loved it. With my two big dogs for company I happily wandered the surrounding hills and explored the many backroads and trails which thread the area. In the winter, my little road was the last to be ploughed out and I was often hours late for work. In northern Ontario there are proper winters which often prevent people from being at work on time. It was never an issue.

Life moves on and eventually I moved closer to town. Now, I was curious to see if the house was still standing and whether the image of it in my memory accorded with reality.

But it wasn't to be. As is so often the case fate intervened with my plans – but I'm getting ahead of myself. Let's back-track a few hours and a few miles.

In Iron Bridge I filled my tank before heading west along the Trans-Canada Highway for a few miles. I'd noticed a road which snaked between Clear and Big Basswood Lakes and led generally in the direction I wanted to be travelling. Signs close to the beginning informed me to be careful as it was an active logging haul road, but as the road followed the Red Rock Lake shore, the hard-packed gravel disappeared, replaced by two narrow lanes of mirror-flat, freshly scraped road, separated by a foot-high berm of new gravel. There were no logging trucks to be seen, but the road-grader was at work preparing the road for the loaded tandem-trucks which would soon be using it. And it wasn't long before I caught up to him.

1972 Moto Guzzi Eldorado
Packed and ready for adventure

Getting the bike across the loose pile to get by proved far easier than I anticipated. I slowed to a crawl, angled the bike at forty-five degrees and rode. The front wheel ploughed a little, there was a tinkle of small rocks hitting the metal sump, but in less than a second I was in the 'left lane' riding on. Further on, I crossed back onto the other side, shortly before the freshly-graded section ended. I found myself thinking, 'if all the roads across to Dunn's Valley are like this it will be no problem at all'. As I soon found out, they weren't, and it was.

Soon after the freshly-graded area the road turned into a muddy track, heading due north within the broad floodplain of the Mississagi River. The road – if I can call it that – had become a narrow scar between endless swampy forest, the road bed awash with large puddles, soft sand and stretches of hard mud. In places I could see where transverse logs – the old corduroy road – had been used to 'float' the road across the more swampy areas. I could tell from the tracks that nobody had been down the road for many days. I would have at least expected to see four-wheeler tracks. There were none.

Nevertheless, the Eldo and I danced around the puddles we could avoid splashing through, took it slowly through the muddy sections and carried on. 'This ain't so bad', I thought, using my best Grammar School English, 'as long as it stays like this, it will be fine'.

After a couple of miles, the road turned abruptly west. I stopped to check the map on my phone, slipped the bike into first gear, and…nothing. No gear. I tried again. Still nothing. Oh joy. In the middle of nowhere and the gearbox decides to act up. I pushed the pedal down for a third time, the gear engaged and we were on our way. This aberration was never repeated for the whole of the rest of the journey. I sometimes wonder whether the Eldorado has a vengeful spirit or a warped sense of humour. Perhaps it's her way of complaining about the abuse I subject her too and she does these things to knock the edges off my overweening confidence.

Almost immediately, the road began a shallow climb up the valley edge and the road surface changed to river gravel and cobbles embedded in greasy clay. The grass growing down the centre did nothing to assure me that the road was in frequent use, and, of course, by this point I was well beyond cell-phone service. Ahead, I could see that the recent thunderstorm had washed a gully across the track, and in trying to avoid this deep divot, the line I chose plunged my front wheel into a narrow wheel rut. Before I could react, the front wheel slid sideways and I was lying against the bank, my foot trapped beneath the bike.

I quickly leaned forwards and switched off. I didn't need the Eldorado churning away beneath me as I tried to extricate myself from this little 'whoops'. My right foot was pinioned between the soft pannier and the bank so I tried to pull it free. Nope. I put my left foot on the seat, braced against the bank and was able to move the bike just enough that I could slide my foot out. All this happened in less time than it took to read these words, and I was soon standing in the road, heaving to get the bike back on its wheels. It might have been a different story if the Eldorado had been right over on its side, but since it was propped at about forty-five degrees against the bank, it was a simple job to put some weight on the footrest and haul it upright. Apart from a little mud neither the bike not I were any the worse for wear.

Finding neutral, starting the bike again, then pushing it out of the slimy rut by feeding power to the rear wheel while I staggered alongside took a little effort, but soon enough I was able to remount and carry on. Would there be more of these incidents? I hoped not.

It was only another two or three miles across to the junction with the Chapleau Highway – two or three miles of puddles, rocks, gravel and mud – but eventually I reached the tarmac again without busting the sump on the larger rocks or sliding off into the forest. I checked my map again. A couple of miles on the paved highway would bring me to Wharncliffe. After that, it looked as though another small road worked its way generally west to Dunn's Valley. Would this be more of the same or a more well-travelled route?

At first, it looked like the latter. There were a few houses scattered beside the road and some rudimentary paving. Soon enough though, the paving ended and it was back to the familiar mix of gravel, cobbles, puddles, rock and potholes for the next five miles before the road dropped back down into the floodplain of the Mississagi River and the road became dead straight line across a flat, forested sand plain. Sand is never my favourite to ride on, but, apart from a few damp and rutted patches, the going was firm and even moderately smooth. It wasn't a place to race though. Occasionally wet grooves would tug at the front wheel, but by staying loose and keeping my speed down, we got through to Dunn's Valley unscathed.

The community of Dunn's Valley consists of…well, actually, not very much at all. A large hand-written sign at the intersection of Moose Street and Goose Street (also hand-written signs) declared:

"This is Dunn's Valley, population just a few, weekends, a few more."

A few houses and small farmsteads are scattered along the roads, lying within the flat lands of the Wannamaker Creek valley, but there is nothing one can identify as a community core. Precipitous bedrock cliffs overlook the valley. I'm a sucker for a good bit of rock, so I pulled over at the creek bridge to take a picture of the vertical, spruce clad granite, before moving off towards Ophir and the little road which leads to my former home.

Life is full of minor disappointments. Where, decades ago, I used to stop to let my dogs out of the car to race me the mile to the farmhouse, was a large sign saying that the road was closed. Apparently the bridge was under repair and the valley was inaccessible – at least from this end. I suppose, had I been truly motivated to see my former home, I could have circled round through Havilah and got at it that way, but the moment had passed. I rode on.

We can be fairly sure that the biblical realm of Ophir, famous for providing King Solomon with gold, ivory, sandalwood, peacocks, frankincense and monkeys was not located in northern Ontario. Nevertheless, at the end of the nineteenth century there were clearly a few who thought they'd found their pot of gold at the end of the rainbow, naming the Ophir (Havilah) mine after the old testament mythical kingdom.

Possibly not the Old Testament Kingdom of Ophir

At first, small scale mining operations proved successful with high gold yields per ton of ore processed, but as so often the case with mines within the fractured and complex Canadian Shield, much of the gold proved difficult and uneconomic to mine. Despite promising beginnings, by the nineteen twenties, operations had virtually ceased. Of the little community of Ophir, which had once housed the mine workers, very little now remains. I counted a total of three houses, one of which was collapsing.

After a short side trip to Poplar Dale, where I'd once briefly worked at the Asam's sawmill, mainly to see the two elderly brothers working with their horses, I stopped at the side of the road to check a few things on the bike before starting the long ride home. Stopping at the side of the road in deeply rural northern Ontario is a dangerous business. No sooner had I pulled over and extracted a large channel-lock wrench from my tail-bag to check and tighten my exhaust (I didn't actually need it), when an ancient and frail-looking lady pulled up alongside to ask if I needed any help. I am not a small person, and I was dressed in a heavy leather jacket and mud-covered leather chaps, and holding a large metal tool in my hands, yet this kindly lady fully wound down her window to make sure I was OK. I explained I was just doing a little checking before setting out for home, thanked her for stopping and she drove away, leaving me to my roadside fiddling. She'd barely gone out of sight when a middle-aged couple in a pickup truck drew along-side, slowing, window down. I quickly signed that all was well, and as they drove away, I stowed my tools and got rolling. I could see that if I'd had any serious maintenance to do, I would have spent more time talking and explaining to generous and helpful people, than managing to get anything fixed.

Since I'd got an early start to the day, it was still only an hour or two after lunchtime as I started to head for home. I was in no rush. Once I joined Highway 17 heading east, I settled in at a comfortable speed, perfectly content to watch those in a hurry rush past. The likelihood was that I would see them again at the next gas station, coffee shop or road works, since speeding on the highway rarely translates into getting anywhere faster than anyone else.

The few snacks that lingered in my raccoon-mauled bag were still untouched, and since I had yet to eat anything that day, I eagerly headed to the Tim Horton's coffee shop in Blind River. Covid restrictions were still in place, but a few, well-spaced tables were available, so I plonked myself down near a window with a coffee and ham and cheese sandwich, to catch up on my phone messages. I like to be able to keep an eye on the bike, not because I'm particularly worried about theft, but I like to see people's reactions to it as they pass. Even non-motorcyclists can tell it's not a modern machine, and with bags and gear strapped all over, and now with a good covering of mud on the side where it fell, its looks suggest interesting travels.

A couple of people snapped pictures with their phones, and one older man did a full three-sixty tour before catching my eye in the window and waving excitedly. It was obvious he wanted to talk, and since I'd finished my sandwich and had some checking and tidying to do on the bike, I went outside carrying the rest of my coffee.

These bike-side conversations often follow the same pattern: 'what year is the bike, where are you heading, where have you come from?' followed by wistful stories of their own motorcycle trips, decades ago, before family and work responsibilities intruded.

I'm happy to listen. If I've been feeling tired or dispirited, their nostalgic tales always revive my flagging spirits, and I would set off with renewed enthusiasm and vigour, even if my shoulders were aching and my rear end was numb.

Fortunately, that wasn't the case when I left Blind River. I still had plenty of energy, the weather was pleasant and I'd already decided that I would treat myself to a lazy night in a motel, rather than beat myself up with an epic marathon back to home.

While I was filling up with fuel once again, I heard a couple of motorcyclists talking about how glad they were that they'd followed some third party's advice and taken the Lee Valley Road from Espanola, avoiding a huge section of road works along the Trans-Canada Highway. I knew the Lee Valley Road. I'd ridden it with my friend Ken a couple of years earlier, so as I saw the beginning of the road works at Massey, I turned right and was rewarded with twenty miles of pleasant, empty road instead of spending an undetermined amount of time, sitting in a line of idling traffic, waiting for the flag man to signal us through.

By the time I got to Sturgeon Falls I was entirely happy to stop for the day. It hadn't been the longest day's riding I'd ever done, but with the pleasant ride along the Little White River, the low speed excitement of the unpaved backroads and then the long haul east along the Trans-Canada Highway, I was well and truly ready for a rest by late afternoon. I pulled in to the Lincoln Motel, paid the pleasant young lady at the front desk, received my key to the nice, clean room, and settled back to watch some drivel on TV. It can't have been very engaging. I can no longer remember what I was watching.

The following morning I was soon heading south on the four-lane Highway 11, rather surprised to find myself slightly chilled by the cool morning air. Four-lane highways are not my natural habitat. I tend to avoid them if at all possible. They are boring and tedious and if there are more engaging ways to get from A to B I'd rather use them.

Unfortunately, in this part of the world, the options are limited by the scale of the geography and the sparseness of the population. No one has seen fit to plaster the landscape with a multitude of scenic byways, so I was stuck heading in the general direction of Toronto for the next eighty miles.

The Eldorado is an elderly girl. She'll be fifty next year. Part of me wonders whether it's not a bit cruel to run her for hours at highway speeds. Then I listen to the sound of the engine, humming contentedly at around 4000 rpm and right in the middle of the torque curve, and forget about worrying. She feels relaxed, smooth and happy to drone along at sixty-five or seventy until my backside can't stand it any longer or she starts to stumble for lack of fuel. Rock strewn and puddle-soaked backroads, winding country lanes, major thoroughfares – the old girl handles them all with dignity and poise. She truly is a great all-rounder: a true ADV bike.

As I neared Huntsville the sun had brought a little warmth to the air and my initial chill was fading, so by the time I was heading along delightful roads towards Haliburton and Bancroft, I was warm, comfortable and enjoying myself.

Sometimes riding roads you've ridden many times before can be tedious. Your mind lurches ahead to the next destination while your body is left behind to claw its way through the landscape, mile by mile. But even though the roads I was riding were very familiar, I was enjoying every moment. It was as if I was seeing the world anew: enchanted where the road mirrored a lake shore, delighted by the marshes and swamps, the farms and farm fields sandwiched between the hills, the mellow bellow of the

Guzzi's pipes a constant accompaniment, but muted by my earplugs. It was a joyful day.

I stopped a few times to take some pictures – a rocky lakeshore here, a waterlily filled wetland there – more for the momentary pleasure of standing quietly looking at the world, than because I had any specific use for the pictures.

Along the road heading to Haliburton

I stopped again a few miles further on. I'd seen a perfect, unoccupied pull-off next to the lake shore. I couldn't think of a more delightful place to eat the remaining peanuts, crisps and biscuits my nighttime raider had failed to devour.

Two hours later I wheeled the Eldorado into the garage, turned off the fuel tap and shed my riding gear. I was just about to say that the journey had been completely free of mechanical issues but that wouldn't be telling the whole truth. While I was camped, I'd pulled the valve cover off the right cylinder to cure a microscopic, but nonetheless irritating leak that had been spotting my pant leg with tiny flecks of oil. A few moments with the allen keys, a thin smear of silicone and it was totally cured and I was fleck-free for the rest of the journey. There'd been no need for plug or points cleaning, no need to adjust the carburator, nothing fell off or vibrated to pieces and the Eldorado was running and idling as sweetly at the end of the trip as at the beginning. Darn thing is becoming too reliable. Next time, perhaps I need to take something even older, even more 'stone age'. I know, I have just the thing.

Heading home

THE PANTHER RIDES AGAIN

If you ride a lot, inevitably you find you are going over the same territory time after time. My searches to find unridden roads have grown longer and longer, to the point that I now have to ride a considerable distance before I can start exploring completely new ground.

Yet, as long as you have some different bikes at your disposal, there is value in going over the same old roads as it gives you a chance to evaluate how each bike performs under well-known circumstances.

With these thoughts in mind, I wheeled the Panther out of the garage with the intension of taking it on its longest ride yet. Over the previous few weeks I had ridden it on my normal sixty mile loop a number of times, stopping every few miles to check for loose nuts and bolts, listen carefully to the engine, check the chains – all the things you do to make sure nothing is about to fly loose or land you in a ditch. Apart from still drooling a few teaspoonsful of oil from the cylinder base gasket, which was unsightly but not worrisome, the bike was performing as well as a nineteen-sixties motorcycle, barely changed from the nineteen thirties, could be expected to perform. As long as you followed the precise starting routine, held your tongue in the corner of your mouth in the right way, and prayed to the appropriate deity, it almost always started first kick.

With a comprehensive tool kit safely tucked away in one of the metal side boxes, a small empty gas can, a litre of oil and my rain suit strapped in a bag on the rack, and my camera stuff in the tank bag, I was ready to roll. But before venturing away from our house, I took a few minutes to play with the forks. On my previous rides I'd noticed that the forks would clunk badly over rough ground - not bottoming out, but a bone-jarring clanging as metal hit against metal.

Ready to roll

It didn't take long before my drain pan was full of dirty ATF, replaced with the appropriate amount of 15/40 oil. It may not have been precisely what was specified in the owner's handbook, but it was what was sitting on the shelf. A couple of pumps on the forks showed a pleasingly stiffer action and I really had to work hard to get any nasty noises. Good enough. Let's roll.

A quick peek inside the gas tank assured me that I had enough fuel to get to the first gas station in Westport, a mere twenty-five miles away. I still had no idea how quickly or slowly the Panther gobbled fuel. For that matter, I didn't even know how much fuel I could cram into the tank, so one of today's challenges was to explore the Panther's range.

When it first starts, the Panther likes to buck and

wheeze. The carburetor slide is loose enough in the body that it audibly clicks when the bike is idling, and makes the mixture sufficiently erratic that, until the engine is warm, it burps and farts its way down the road. Fortunately, it warms up quickly and soon we were gliding along serenely heading north. Serenely? Well, perhaps not that. Agreeably then.

Large capacity single cylinder motorbikes designed as daily transportation for the financially challenged are not noted for their smoothness. This is no Velocette Venom or race-tuned Matchless G50. Counterbalance shaft? Forget it. Rubber mounted engine? Not a chance. The large metal bits thrashing about inside the engine cases send their messages right through the frame. At idle, the front wheel dances a little jig in perfect syncopation with the piston. At higher speeds, those vibrations make their way to the rider through the handlebars, foot pegs and seat. They are not unpleasant, but constant, changing pitch and frequency with road and engine speed.

First gear arrives with the grinding sound of large cogs doing their best to mesh, but subsequent changes, whether up or down can be quiet, as long as you're not in a rush. These are not Honda gears. A light tap with the toe will be rewarded either with a mess of neutrals or some serious gnashing of bits. But as long as you blip the throttle and push the long throw lever all the way down, ignoring the resistance in the middle, the next gear will engage smoothly. That's a relative term. There is nothing smooth about these bikes, other than their delicious appearance.

Anyway, we're underway. The idea is to get into top gear as soon as possible and stay there. With a massively heavy flywheel, Panthers were designed to lug, so taking a corner at anything above about twenty-five miles an hour, you may as well stay in top gear and just roll on the throttle.

Acceleration won't warp your eyeballs but you'll get there eventually.

I'm not going to pretend that it miraculously smooths out once you reach cruising speed, but at an indicated 55mph (about 52 actual) it hums along, feeling unstressed, and the vibrations which filter through your whole body feel more organic than mechanical. It will happily cruise at an indicated 60 too and I've even seen higher speeds on the needle, but, by then, it's definitely out of its comfort zone. This is a bike that was designed for lugging around a heavy sidecar at lower rates of progress. It's more diesel than Ducati, and deserves to be treated accordingly.

Occasionally, while riding, I look down at the engine to check on how much oil is leaking. The persistent leak at the cylinder base starts after about ten miles then continues as long as the engine is running. A couple of trails work their way across the snout of the sump but they barely even dampen a rag as I wipe them off. It is enough that I keep a constant eye on it, but not worrying enough to make me want to curtail my ride.

Some days are just made for riding, and this was one of them. It was warm, but not too warm, with a little hazy cloud to take the sting out of the summer sun, and being Monday, the roads were virtually traffic free. Every few minutes a car or truck would pass in the other direction, but most of the time I had no other vehicles in sight and was able to bumble along just where the Panther felt at its most relaxed. With the wide handlebars and the footpegs set low, the seating position is just about perfect.

By the time I reached the gas station in Westport I was already feeling settled in and ready for a full day's ride. Before long I was through Westport, chugging up the optimistically named 'Mountain Road' towards Bolingbroke and the Crow Lake Road leading to Sharbot Lake. From time to time I would lean over to check on the oil leak, but it was never more than a dribble or two on the crankcase.

The miles began to add up. I sailed through Ardoch and Plevna and was soon rolling up the Buckshot Lake Road heading for the tiny hamlets of Vennachar and Matawatchan. If you've read any of my other books, those names may seem familiar as I often come this way and have described them more fully in other chapters. If not, never fear – you're not missing much. Although they were once much larger settlements they have shriveled to almost nothing and it's easy to pass by and barely notice their existence.

I only mention Matawatchan because, as I turned the corner heading for Camel Chute and the road to Calabogie I was suddenly deep into roadworks. There was no question that this was being done by the local township. The former road surface had been ripped to shreds, there was nobody on duty to flag you through, there was active machinery everywhere, and we were expected to navigate a single incredibly rough lane, composed of jagged blocks of ripped tarmac.

I had barely started bouncing my way through when I saw a truck coming along the same narrow track from the other direction. I pulled as far to the side as I could without rolling off into the ditch, but the truck driver had had the same thought and pulled over, putting two of his wheels onto the active berm, leaving just enough space for me to pass.

This may sound as though I'm complaining about the township's cavalier attitude to health and safety, but actually, it was rather fun. It was definitely a case of local lads getting on with the job with little concern for the formalities. With so little traffic to worry about, they hadn't made any provision for casual passer's-though like me. We had to muddle along, dodging backhoes, rollers and trucks.

The roadworks section was, mercifully, quite short and in no time the Panther was rolling down the hill leading towards the Madawaska River and the Centennial Lake Road which hugs its shore. Barely any time had passed since I'd ridden this road on both my Moto Guzzi Eldorado and my Suzuki Cavalcade, so I was able to make some interesting comparisons. Both the Eldo and the Cade are capable of much higher speeds than the Panther, yet I was amused to find that I was riding at roughly the same speed I always do. Unlike the twerp on the sportbike who was traveling far too fast and I'd seen almost lose it on a corner the last time I was on that road, I tend to hum along in the general vicinity of the speed limit, enjoying the sun glistening off the water, the jagged austerity of the numerous rock-cuts and the heady smell of pine and cedar wafting from the adjacent forest.

Summer is road maintenance season in Canada so I wasn't too surprised to encounter another long section where the asphalt had been removed and a new bed of gravel had been laid. The contrast between the two areas couldn't have been more profound. This area was well signed and the gravel surface was perfectly smooth and recently rolled. Riding was as effortless as if it had been paved. I was following someone in an SUV who was clearly intimidated by the gravel surface. Had I been on one of the other bikes I would have overtaken, but the Panther has only so much to give, so I hung back and plodded along until the paving reappeared and, suddenly regaining some courage, the SUV disappeared in the distance.

At the lakeside park in Calabogie, I pulled over to check my oil. The front of the engine was streaked with little rivulets of oil, but the level in the sump was essentially unchanged. Oil leaks can be deceptive. Even a tiny amount can look like a major disaster, especially if you're used to modern bikes which aren't supposed to leak at all.

South of Calabogie I was humming along quite happily when suddenly I felt a misfire. There, it happened again, and continued to reoccur for the next few miles. It had little effect on performance but was slightly unnerving. Was there a whisker of dirt on the plug, perhaps? After a few more miles the occasional stutter seemed to disappear and before I knew it, I pulled in to the gas station in Westport again to check my fuel level. Since I'd filled up I'd ridden the best part of two hundred miles, yet there was still more than enough fuel in the tank to get me home.

Back in the garage I checked the bike over, looking for loose or missing bolts and any other signs of distress, finding only one. A small retaining bolt where the electronic ignition hides within the old magdyno casing had gone AWOL, allowing the case plate to move slightly. This minor movement must have been enough to throw the timing out for a few moments, allowing the stumbles. A quick search of my parts bin for a suitable bolt, a dab of thread-locker and the bike was back to normal.

I was thrilled. I'd had so many ups and downs with the Panther that it felt wonderfully liberating to finally believe I had an old bike on my hands that I could actually use.

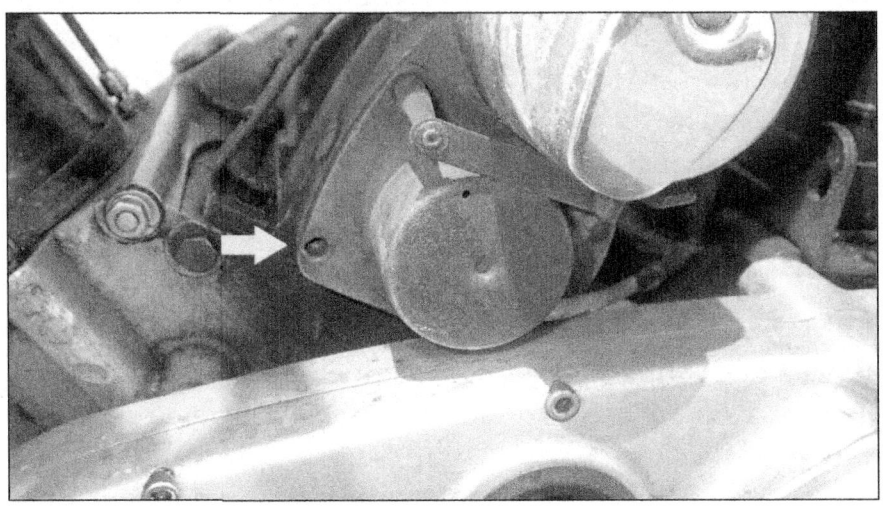

A few days later I summoned the energy and enthusiasm to address the cylinder base leak. When I lifted the cylinder, I could see the gasket was still in excellent condition, so, rather than tear the whole engine apart again, I cleaned up all the mating surfaces, smeared the thinnest amount of silicone gasket sealant, making sure not to block the critical oil hole at the rear of the cylinder, and bolted it back together.

A quick ride around my ten mile test loop showed no leakage, so the following Sunday I crossed my fingers for good luck and rode eighty miles before breakfast. And it didn't leak. What? Not at all? Well, no – not from the cylinder base anyway. It still throws one or two tiny spots from one of the timing case bolts, and sooner or later I'll get around to sealing that too, but hey, it wouldn't be a British bike if it didn't shed a little lubricant.

Now, where's my road atlas.

THE FRANKENBEAST[9]

Once upon a time, in a country far, far away, a shiny new 1970 Triumph Bonneville rolled off the Meriden production line and ended up in Canada. No doubt in those early days, it was someone's pride and joy, kept spotless, and only ridden when the sun was shining, and the roads were dry.

As the years went by, we can imagine that the paint faded, rust spots appeared on the nuts and chrome, and the bike lost its lustre. Perhaps it lingered in a shed for a while. Perhaps it was dropped, parked, and ignored, its carbs becoming gummy and its tank full of stale fuel. Sadly, such things happen – even to the best motorcycles. It probably changed hands a few times, moving from one storage place to the next, gradually losing value and gaining patina, as new, efficient, virtually maintenance-free bikes from the East replaced it in the hearts and minds of its owners.

Stripped of its original tank, mudguards and trim, it gained a new custom fibreglass tank and matching fibreglass oil tank, a fancy new tailpiece containing the battery and sundry electrical bits, plastic mudguards and a

---

[9] A version of this was originally published in 'RealClassic' magazine No. 207)

heavily chromed set of dual exhausts. I am reliably informed that in this condition it was trailered around to various shows where, astonishingly, it was awarded a number of trophies – perhaps more out of pity, than in recognition of its aesthetic appeal. Some attention was paid to the internal bits – pistons, valves etc. were replaced – so it functioned well enough to start and run. But perhaps it's a good thing that the proud owner seemed to have been more interested in showing his creation, than riding it very far. But more of that later.

When it came into Doug's hands, it looked pretty enough – in a garish eighties, pseudo café-racer kind of way - but it soon became apparent that looks can be deceiving. It vibrated. The fibreglass fuel tank leaked, and it would shed pieces whenever he rode it. The screw-in valve adjustment covers were particularly prone to making a getaway, accompanied by the inevitable oil spray before their absence was noticed.

Back in the days before Doug became a responsible family man with a mortgage, a steady partner and now, a delightful daughter, we used to meet up each Sunday morning at Bob's Diner in Delta for breakfast. I was usually on one of my Guzzis. Doug would turn up on whatever calamity he was riding at the time. We would meet, drink coffee, eat and chat, then go our separate ways. One day, during a spirited run on the way home, Doug's Triumph seized. Not a full lock-up – just enough of an internal squeeze to let him know that things were far from healthy inside the Triumph's cases. It was time for some major surgery.

Sometimes what seems like a disaster can actually be a blessing. Doug's good friend Matt is an excellent mechanic with his own small but highly respected auto-repair garage. He and Doug stripped the Triumph completely, finding all kinds of nasties inside, principal of which was pistons which were a size too large for the bores. No wonder it seized. Matt, being a perfectionist, balanced the crank, replaced all the original crankcase and bottom end bearings, and rebored the cylinders, fitting them with new, matching pistons. Doug had been having trouble keeping the twin carbs balanced and in tune, so they sourced a single carb cylinder head from a Triumph Tiger, bought a new Amal carburetor and bolted it all back together. At the same time, the twin exhausts were replaced with Siamese pipes exiting into a single megaphone on the right side.

The fibreglass oil tank was rapidly following the fuel tank's lead by splitting and leaking, so it was replaced with a large capacity cylindrical unit that fits neatly beneath the seat – the extra capacity providing a little more cooling for those hot, Ontario summer days. I have some photographs from a few years ago, which may be visible somewhere close by, which show the Triumph part way through its evolution to its current form. The fibreglass tank has been replaced with a massive aluminium one, but the oil tank and ugly battery tail box – proudly displaying 'T120' – are still in place. It is a shame I don't have any photographs of it in its original 'custom' form, but one look at that tail piece should be enough to convince you of it its former commanding elegance and style.

Nowadays, the battery is tucked in beneath the oil tank. The tail piece has been replaced with a single rear trailer light, bolted on upside down so that it also illuminates the licence plate. The seat is a custom job, made and covered by one of Doug's many friends. In an uncharacteristic nod to safety, Doug has added some miniscule turn signals operated by a switch on the left-hand bar. But despite this concession to modern riding conditions, Doug's approach to motorcycle maintenance and safety would be enough to give any Health and Safety jobsworth[10] alopecia.

[10] British slag: (from Urban Dictionary: *A low ranking official who follows their instructions and procedure to the letter - often just to piss you off and to make them feel important.*

The fuel tank is held on with zip ties. The oil tank is connected with jubilee clips (hose clamps to our trans-Atlantic readers), the speedo cable is held in place with duct tape, and the rear tyre is almost bald. The exhaust is held to the frame with an automotive pipe clamp and a piece of metal that was twisted in a vice. Even the single mirror is a re-purposed bar end item, jury-rigged onto the clutch lever. Amazingly, the brakes both work quite well, the wheel bearings are sound, and the steering isn't notchy. As Doug says himself,

"It's not exactly a shining, beautiful example – but it's sort-of medium safe."

With those comforting words of encouragement, we wheeled it out of his garage and started it up. I would be lying if I told you it started first kick because it didn't. Doug had forgotten to switch the little ignition switch with lies between the tach and speedo into the 'on' position. But somewhat to my surprise, it did start second kick, and soon settled into a steady idle, sounding far less like the bag of rusty bolts I remembered from my earlier encounters with the bike at Bob's diner. There clearly is some value to having someone who actually knows what they are doing to rebuild your engine, as this one was running smoothly with far less mechanical clatter than I was expecting.

Doug lives on an unpaved road near the St. Lawrence River. It is the old road between Montreal and Toronto, now bypassed by the smooth and pleasantly paved St. Lawrence Parkway. Each Spring, as the frozen gravel gradually thaws in the sunshine, the top inch or so of road surface turns to a soupy mush. While it would be stretching the truth to suggest that Doug's bike is ever pristine, the combination of salty road splatter and flash-rusting make it look far more disreputable than it really is.

While the bike idled, I pulled on my gear and straddled it. Although it was running nicely, I decided I had better see if I could start it myself, before venturing too far, so I switched off, folded the foot peg up and the kickstart out, switched the ignition on and gave it a boot. This is no Panther! It kicked over easily and was soon running again, spooling up enthusiastically with the slightest twist of the throttle. Doug's steeply sloping gravel driveway was a first gear job. I controlled downward progress with compression and the rear brake, and I was soon gathering speed along the Old River Road. Because the road was rutted and slimy in patches, I trickled along in second gear, getting used to the feel of the engine. The left side brake and right-side gear change felt normal. The reversed gear lever meant that it was up for first and down for the other three – the same as my Panther.

Despite the reach across that enormous aluminum tank, the riding position was surprisingly comfortable. I was sitting low in the bike, my knees comfortably bent with my feet slightly to the rear, and a slight lean to the flat bars. While the road surface occasionally grabbed and shook the front wheel, Doug's Triumph felt stable, predictable, and completely controllable. It might look like a dog's breakfast but it didn't ride like one.

At the Parkway I turned on to the paved road and accelerated, rather surprised at how eagerly the engine propelled the bike through the gears and the speed with which I reached cruising velocity. The Parkway is regularly patrolled by the folks in blue, so I kept the speed within range of the official limit. At sixty miles an hour the engine was spinning smoothly at around 4000 rpm, with surprisingly little vibration through the bars. Another gear might have been nice, but Doug has plans to change sprockets to knock a few rpm's off the engine at highway speed. Acceleration seemed about the same as my 850 Guzzi, the Triumph's smaller, 650cc engine producing less power while hauling considerably less weight. In a flat-out race I wouldn't know which I would bet on. It would be a close thing.

I have never ridden a classic Triumph before so have

no way of comparing the experience of riding Doug's bike with a more standard Bonneville. I've heard uncharitable things said about some Triumph frames. I don't know whether that would apply to Doug's bike which felt nimble and steered accurately. If its high-speed cornering ability is suspect, with the way I ride, I'm never likely to experience it, and certainly didn't on this day.

When it came time to turn around, I encountered the one fly in the ointment. Whether a couple of plates were sticking or whether it just needed some adjustment, I don't know, but the clutch was a beast[11]. It was fine while switching gears on the move, but trying to navigate at low speed by feathering it resulted in frog hops as I struggled to find a happy place between fully out and fully in. Doug says he's used to it. But if you're Doug, you can get used to just about anything.

I didn't go too far on this little test ride – just far enough to get a sense of the bike. I was quite ready to be terrified – after all, it is a bit of a Frankenbeast – but found it surprisingly comfortable and pleasant to ride. Whenever I'm riding an unfamiliar bike I always ask myself, "Is this a bike I could ride all day?" since getting anywhere in a country like Canada usually involves such feats of endurance, and, for me at least, short rides seem a bit pointless. Doug's Triumph felt smooth, comfortable, and robust. "Yes," I answered myself. "I could."

As I headed back down the Parkway then along the soft surface of Old River Road I was once again reminded that before the days of ADV bikes, all bikes were expected to be competent and manageable when road conditions

---

[11] Doug informs me that after a minor adjustment, the clutch is working smoothly.

were less than perfect. Doug's Triumph certainly lived up to those expectations. It tracked well, felt completely stable and was unperturbed by sudden changes in the road surface.

By the time I pulled into his shed, my brown leather hiking boots were completely grey and the bike was covered in gravel slop. Did Doug care? Not at all. He might give the Bonneville a wipe over with an oily rag one of these days, but I wouldn't hold your breath. Doug's Triumph might look like a rolling disaster, but it's ready to go at a moment's notice.

ONE MAN'S MEAT

The other day, chat on one of the motorcycle forums I inhabit went down the Honda PC800 (Pacific Coast) worm hole. If ever there was a bike which divides opinion this is it. On the one hand some motorcyclists love the bodywork, the ease of cleaning, the utility of the built-in luggage, the weather protection, the funky looks and the smooth, hidden mechanicals, while the majority despise it as a two-wheeled Honda Civic, a plastic scooter – too sanitized, not enough motorcycle.

Perhaps a little description is in order. In 1989 Honda launched the Pacific Coast as a motorcycle designed to appeal to car drivers. Unlike most motorbikes where styling is usually centred around the visual appeal of the engine, the Pacific Coast completely hid its 800cc V-twin, five speed transmission and shaft drive beneath acres of smooth plastic bodywork. Underneath those panels was a fairly conventional motorcycle, although by designing in automatic hydraulic valve and cam chain adjustment and by rubber mounting the engine, the working bits were smooth and virtually maintenance free.

The front wheel was partially enclosed behind a cowling which completely covered the front disks. The rider and passenger accommodations were spacious and well protected from the weather behind a tall windscreen and lower panels with built-in tip-over protectors, and the tubby rear trunk, hinged to reveal two capacious storage areas was far more scooter-like than anything you'd find on a conventional motorcycle. It was practical and user-friendly.

While the PC800 wasn't a complete flop, it never gained the sales success Honda hoped for and it was dropped from their line-up in 1990, re-emerging in 1994 to struggle on for another few years. There was nothing inherently wrong with the bike – indeed, while not appealing much to mainstream motorcycle buyers, over the years they have proven to be generally reliable and trouble free. In other words, it was a typical Honda product.

In recent years, as used Pacific Coasts prices have fallen, they have developed a cult following among those secure enough in their own identity to ride something which is almost certain to attract curiosity and opinion whenever it's parked.

And that's where I come in. Ever since I saw my first Pacific Coast I'd mentally added it to the list of slightly odd and usual motorbikes that appeal to me, along with such ugly ducklings as the Maico Mobil scooter and the mechanically weird Puch 'Twingle'. My main motorbikes are Moto Guzzis, which are unusual enough for most people, but the Pacific Coast and their ilk are unusual in a completely different order of magnitude.

From time to time I'd see a 'Coast' on the road but had never had the opportunity to examine one closely, or better still, take one for a ride. Then my friend Norm acquired one. Norm is on a life-long challenge to own and briefly ride just about every motorbike ever made – at least, that's how it seems - so I wasn't entirely surprised that something as obscure as the Pacific Coast should end up gracing his garage. It turns out that Norm had briefly dallied with the idea of buying one when they were new, but had decided against it, believing that his riding buddies would laugh at him. Like me, he had been attracted to the Pacific Coast and had nurtured that longing for more than twenty years.

This particular bike had been languishing, unused, in storage belonging to our Sunday morning breakfast restaurateur. Norm bought it cheap to see if he could get it running (of course he could), cleaned it up until it looked almost new, then proudly brought it round so I could have a good look.

It was immaculate. It barely looked as though it had ever been used, its curvy white and grey bodywork – some wags call it Tupperware – gleaming gently in the autumn sun. It was everything I'd hoped for: weird looking, practical to a fault, a bit rare, and about as far from a loud-pipe Harley on the motorcycle spectrum as you could get. It was socially responsible. It was unintimidating. The whole rear end lifted up, exposing a cavernous luggage space, large enough to contain enough groceries for a week or at least a dozen German Shepherd puppies. Did I mention weird?

"Would you like to take it for a spin?" You bet!

I had to suck the saliva back into my mouth because I was starting to drool. Norm handed me the key, I stuck it in the ignition and pressed the starter. The bike immediate started and sat whirring quietly as I put on my helmet and zipped my jacket. Somewhere under all that plastic, an 800cc V-twin was idling, but you'd hardly know it, it's rubber engine mounts made its reciprocations almost undetectable.

I selected first gear – typically Honda smooth – and pulled away. At low speed it felt surprisingly heavy. For some reason I had expected it to be light and easy to throw around but it was no different to any other 600 plus pound motorbike. Accelerating away through the gears it moved off well enough, getting up to cruising speed smoothly and without fuss or undue noise. The triangle between the bars, seat and foot pegs was comfortably neutral and the sound from the exhaust was muted. It was a bike that one could ride all day without stress or difficulty.

The road I was riding was pleasantly twisty and the Pacific Coast handled the corners perfectly well. It felt controllable, untroubled, even serene as we wafted along. I braked hard and the brakes worked. I accelerated hard and the bike got going faster in a perfectly acceptable and effective way. It didn't try to rip my arms out of their sockets, but it wasn't desperately slow either. There was nothing troubling, unsatisfactory or objectionable here. It was just……..dreary!

Oh how I wanted to fall desperately in love with that bike. It was like having a date with a stunningly beautiful woman only to find that she had the conversational skills of a dugong. It was dull. It was uninteresting. It had all the charisma of a two-wheeled Honda Civic. No amount of practicality and sexy bodywork could overcome a tedious riding experience. If Honda had been aiming for a completely neutral, unintimidating, undemanding, almost maintenance free motorbike, they'd hit the nail right on the head. It just didn't grab me.

I did a u-turn, careful not to drop the Pacific Coast onto its cleverly moulded bump strips and returned the bike to Norm, who rode off, tooting au revoir with a pathetic bleat of the horn. Two weeks later it was gone from his garage, replaced by something with a bit more vivacity. I can't say I was desperately surprised.

SOME RANDOM THOUGHTS

This short section might irritate a few people, but tough luck. These are a few of the things which irk me and you are free to agree or disagree as you see fit.

In the motorcycling world, one sees some sad things from time to time, but few things seem more pitiable to me than advertisements offering a bike for sale because (cue whiny voice): 'I don't have anyone to ride with'

Piloting a motorcycle is fundamentally a solo activity. Why then, do so many people seem unable to ride their bikes unless they're part of a convoy? I just don't get it.

We've all seen them. Huge gaggles of almost identical bikes rolling along the highway like a giant centipede – in North America it's usually Harleys or other big cruisers with the obligatory loud pipes and mindless revving at stop lights – either travelling at mind-numbingly slow speed, clogging the road for miles, or trying to pass everyone. An invading army of insurance salesmen, tire fitters, school teachers and truck drivers in their stupid coal-scuttle, pseudo-nazi helmets, hopping from one coffee shop to the next but never really going anywhere, all trying to give the impression that they're the 'Wild Bunch'.

In the UK it's often sport bikes, but the same drone mentality still applies.

I had the dubious pleasure to encounter one such group of cruisers while riding home from a lengthy circuit of northern Ontario on the Moto Guzzi Nuovo Falcone I used to own. The NF is a slow bike. It's happiest rolling along between 50 and 55 mph so I wasn't surprised to hear the roar of half a dozen bikes charging by. Half an hour later I passed them as they sat fueling up, only to be passed again a few minutes later. Needless to say, I was invisible because I wasn't on a 'real' motorbike. I kept plodding along. Further on, there they were again, drinking coffee outside a Tim Hortons. This happened a couple of more times until they no longer passed me. I assume they returned home after their exciting group ride, telling tales of their adventures.

I'm as sociable as the next guy – I'll ignore the sniggering – and I often meet up with a few friends for breakfast, but we all arrive separately, chat for a while, then go our different ways. Very occasionally I might ride a few miles with one or two others, and even more rarely, I have ridden multi-day trips with another rider. But it's not my favourite thing and I generally avoid it.

Riding with someone else is an exercise in compromise. If you're following, there is an expectation that you'll match their speed and whether they like to ride more quickly or more slowly than you, you are no longer riding your own ride. If they're too fast, you may quickly find yourself in over your head. Too slow and the frustration builds, leading to erratic riding or inattention. As we all know, unless you're riding your own ride, your chances of ending up in the accident ward rise exponentially. Too often you see or hear about groups of riders getting themselves in a pickle because some looney up front has spied an overtaking opportunity which the drones behind inevitably follow.

Sport bike riders seem particularly subject to this kind of lunacy. While driving a rental car in the Highlands of

Scotland a couple of years ago I saw a perfect example of how not to ride. I was stopped awaiting for a break in the oncoming traffic before making a well-signaled, legal turn into a parking area on the other side of the road. A couple of cars behind me had seen my indicator, recognized my intensions and stopped behind me. Just as the opposing traffic cleared and I began to make the turn, I checked my mirror to see three or four road-rockets coming up fast, riding the centreline. Had I completed my turn I would have wiped them all out and they probably would have wiped us out too. The front rider, who was riding far too fast for the conditions, had completely misread the situation and led his followers into extreme danger as they blindly followed his lead. I wonder if they chuckled about it in the pub afterwards. I'll bet they did. Prats!

In the UK, hordes of riders congregate at places like Matlock Bath, parking for hours while they stand around ogling each-other's bikes. I like seeing interesting bikes too but the idea of standing around along the busy A6 in Matlock Bath or anywhere else for that matter, with crowds of others when there are delightful and scenic roads to ride is anathema to me. Especially when this kind of mob mentality inevitably leads to wheelies, burn-outs and other moronic behavior. I'll take the view of a bike from the bike seat, over parked bikes at the roadside any day of the week.

And as for Sturgis, Daytona Bike Week and the other mega-gatherings in the United States. Let's just say there is nothing, absolutely nothing that could induce me to go. They represent everything I find unpleasant, uninteresting and contemptable in the motorcycling world.

While I'm on the subject, I may as well explain my attitude towards the products of Harley Davidson. In Canada, about every second bike you see on the road is a Harley. They are as common as Ford pick-ups, and to me, for that reason alone, about as interesting. On sunny summer days you see them out in droves, resplendent in shiny chrome, leather tassels and absurd monkey bars, their riders splayed out like starfish with their feet barely reaching the 'highway pegs', paddling insecurely with both feet down through intersections, then roaring off, aftermarket pipes bellowing.

Not all, of course. You do see perfectly ordinary people, riding perfectly well on big Harley tourers heading across the country on major trips. And late in the season, when most people have their bikes put away for the winter and it's raining and cold, if I see any bike out on the road, it won't be an ADV bike. It's almost certain to be some grizzled old warrior on a well-used Harley, who's likely to grin and wave whatever I'm riding. But they are the exception, not the rule.

Most – or at least most of the ones I notice – are 'customized'. This means buying shiny bits from the dealer, pulling them out of their plastic wrappers and slapping them on the bike. Fancy brake reservoir and horn covers, bolt on chrome frame trim and fender fittings. If they have skulls or eagle heads, or 'express your bold, renegade attitude'[12], so much the better.

Probably the thing that irks me most – and this doesn't apply to all, or perhaps even most Harley riders – is their brand myopia and their general ignorance of the world of motorcycles beyond their narrow focus. Countless times, Harley riders seeing my Moto Guzzis have struggled with the name and said things like,

"Motogussi – who makes them?". This brand monomania extends to the general, non-riding public who,

---

[12] *Quoted from a Harley advertisement on the web.*

while looking straight at the manufacturer's name on the side of my bike have asked,

"Do Harley make them?" or worse yet,

"You should get a real bike – a Harley."

I suspect Harley Davidson might be delighted by this level of ignorance of anything that wasn't made in Milwaukee. If they were truly the world's best motorcycles, unsurpassed by any other make it would be understandable. But they're not. In the past they had a dismal reliability record, especially during the AMF years of the seventies, and while their bikes have been reasonably sound since, they are no better and no worse than those from other manufacturers.

There is something undeniably seductive about a big, lumbering, low-revving V-twin, cradled in an adequately performing chassis with decent brakes and plenty of space for rider and passenger. Through careful marketing, Harley have nurtured a culture which glorifies Harley, America, weird and ill-considered concepts of 'freedom', and the vague ego-massaging notion of rugged individualism and toxic masculinity which used to be restricted to Marlborough advertisements and John Wayne, and is weirdly conservative and deeply resistant to change.

A few years back they produced what was probably their best-ever engine: a liquid-cooled, double overhead cam beauty developed in conjunction with Porsche. They wasted it by putting it in ludicrous 'urban-cruiser' frames with garish graphics and styling. Needless to say, they were not stunning sales successes, didn't attract the Harley loyalists to the new format, and were soon dropped.

Although I find it loathsome that years ago Harley tried to trademark the distinctive off-beat V-twin sound, I actually like the sound of their bikes – at least, I like the sound of the bikes which haven't been adulterated. Sadly, it seems that many Harley riders feel it's necessary to trash the factory silencers for some obnoxious after-market 'look-at-me' pipes which blare and fart and almost always sound absurd. But I suppose that's the point. The riders want to be noticed. Just the other day I pulled up behind a Harley at an intersection. Even though I was wearing ear plugs he had the radio turned up so loud I could hear Bob Seeger's *'Night Moves'* above the bellow of his aftermarket pipes. As he accelerated hard from the intersection, hands on his monkey bars, his exhausts shaking the nearby windows, he hooked his feet on his highway pegs. Starfish man hits the highway, his wasp-trap pant legs flapping in the wind.

And yet, despite my distain for the 'Harley culture' (if that isn't an oxymoron), three of my best roadside memories involved Harleys. It goes to show that, like many a good novel, what's on the outside doesn't necessarily tell you much about the inside.

INCIDENT 1

I had been out for an early morning ride on my 1972 Moto Guzzi Eldorado. It was a beautiful May Sunday morning. The lilacs were in full bloom and I was enjoying burbling along in the warm air relishing the gently curving road and the mellow sound of the bike. The roads were empty; most people were still in bed. Then it happened. The back of the bike went loose; I had a puncture. Since I was only out for a short ride I hadn't packed any tools or a puncture repair kit, but I had my cell phone in my jacket and my youngest son was at home with his pickup truck. If I gave him a call, he would come and collect me and the bike. He might not even mind too much.

Pushing the bike until I reached a farm field gate, I unzipped my jacket and pulled out the phone. No signal.

The part of Ontario where I live has many black holes where no cell service penetrates. Predictably, I was in one.

After about half an hour a single car rolled by but didn't stop. Another fifteen minutes passed and I was starting to wonder whether I should start walking to see if I could find a signal, or just wait until - well, I wasn't quite sure what - when I heard the distinctive rumble of a bike coming around the bend. Actually, it was two bikes. The first, ridden by a middle aged guy, was a Harley. I'm not sure which model, but it was a touring bike with backrests and bags and a complete absence of skulls. The second, ridden by his partner, was a Hyosung 650.

My poor bike was noticeably sagging in the rear so they couldn't help notice the flat tire as they pulled to a stop.

"Anything we can do to help?" asked the Harley rider.

"It's just a flat. I need to get to somewhere where I can get a cell signal" I responded. "My son has a truck and will come and get me if I can call him. I expect I'll be able to flag a car down eventually".

The lady on the Hyosung lifted her face shield and said, "Jim (I'll call him Jim as I didn't catch his name), you could give him a ride. It'll only be for a few miles."

Jim didn't look thrilled, but he stepped off his bike, removed his rider backrest and stowed it in a pannier before climbing back astride the Harley, indicating for me to do the same. I quickly grabbed and buckled my helmet, pulled the keys from the Eldorado and clambered on.

Soon we were rolling down the road, the Harley pulsing seductively slowly as we eased around the first bend. I'm tall and Jim wasn't so I had a beautifully clear view of the road ahead from the high rear seat. It had been ages since I'd been a passenger. Decades actually. The last time I can recall being on the back of a bike was on a friend's Velocette Venom back in the early nineteen seventies. But you never forget. I settled in, didn't try to steer Jim's bike for him, and enjoyed the ride.

To say I liked the feel of the Harley is an understatement. The big thudding engine seemed to drop down to almost no revs in the corners then chug away as it accelerated out. The sound and feel were delightful and I was almost sad when I could see there were a few bars showing on my phone and it was time to make the call. Jim and his partner left me at an intersection and after I thanked them they rode off to complete their ride.

Alex soon turned up with his truck and my bike ramp and drove me back to where my forlorn Eldorado was parked. Within moments we had it loaded and were on our way home – my mind full of the intoxicating sound and feel of the Harley and the kindness shown by its rider and his partner.

INCIDENT 2

There aren't too many settled places along the Alaska

Highway between Watson Lake and Whitehorse in the Yukon; just a handful of gas station / motels and a couple of tiny communities, so it's a fairly good bet that any bike parked at the side of the road is in trouble. That must have been the thought running through the minds of a couple of fine people from Minnesota as they pulled their Harley to a halt alongside my bike. I have to admit, it was a reasonable assumption on their part, as just at that moment I'd been leaned over in the saddle adjusting the idle mixture on the left-side carburetor on my 46 year old Guzzi and it must have looked as though I was having trouble.

I'd actually stopped to take some pictures of some signs written in cobbles at the side of the road, and, before setting off again, was just playing with the carb settings by ear, searching for that elusive 'perfect' spot where the idling is metronome smooth. I'd switched off and was just about to put my gloves back on when they arrived.

"Is everything OK?" they asked.

Compared to my well-worn, tatty looking bike, with luggage and spare tire held on with a bunch of bungees, their maroon, full dress Ultra Limited was spotless. I could imagine they were thinking that it might be only a matter of time before I was genuinely stuck at the side of the road. We chatted briefly about our riding plans. If they were shocked to hear that I'd made it from Ontario they were far too polite and pleasant to show it, and after once again making sure everything was under control, they rode away. I soon followed. Within a few miles I saw them up ahead so I closed the gap enough that I would be distantly visible in their mirrors then matched their pace. After their kindness in stopping, I didn't want them worrying that I was still back where they'd left me. Once again, Harley riders had a battered down the door of my preconceptions.

A couple of days later I briefly encountered the

Minnesota couple again in Dawson City as they left a coffee shop I was just entering. They were heading further west and north to Alaska while I would be heading up the Dempster Highway. If they were surprised to see I'd made it they didn't let on. Their Harley was still spotless.

INCIDENT 3

On my way home from the Arctic circle I'd been racing a thunderstorm east across the Manitoba prairies when the Eldorado suddenly died. I'd been chasing an erratic misfire for a few thousand miles without any success but the bike had kept on rolling.. Now it was no longer erratic: the bike was dead.

I looked at the towering cloud heading my way. Unless I could get moving quickly I was in for a soaking. Hauling my tools out of my pannier I started to trace the problem, quickly finding a detached electrical lead beneath the fuel tank. Had it just been a lead that had worked loose it would have been the fix of a moment, but annoyingly the brass connector at the coil had rotted through and there was no longer any way to re-attach the lead.

Few a few seconds I was stumped until I remembered that within my little bag of miscellaneous bits, I had a spare coil. I was just in the middle of extracting the coil when I heard that rumble as a large motorbike rode by, braked quickly then turned around to check on me. Once again, my good Samaritan arrived on a Harley.

My bike might have been out of fuel. I might have required a tool I didn't have. I could have been crying out for someone to call for a recovery vehicle for me. He had no idea, but had seen a fellow bike rider in distress and turned around to see if he could help.

Luckily I was well on my way to fixing the problem on my own. He could see my tools all laid out on the road, the coil in my hand and listened attentively as I explained the problem and the fix. Once he was sure I had everything under control, and after I'd thanked him for taking the time to stop, he rode off. I made yet another mental note to myself to always check if I see someone at the side of the road, slapped the spare coil on to the side of the bike with gorilla tape, connected the leads to the right places and was soon on my way. I even managed to stay ahead of the storm.

Despite my distain for some aspects of the 'Harley culture' it's clear that it would be a grievous mistake to assume that everyone who rides Harley motorcycles is ignorant, boorish and annoying. Some are, for sure, but there are many fine people who are attracted to the style, the sound, the feel and the performance of what are, after all, very fine motorcycles.

ON GETTING OFF YOUR BACKSIDE

As I was walking along I'd had a revelation. I was hiking in Frontenac Park – a natural environment park set in the rugged bush of eastern Ontario. This isn't wilderness. You are never more than ten or fifteen miles from the next person, but if you get up early and set out on one of the back-country trails you can have the place to yourself.

The trails are well marked but little more than a slightly worn groove in the forest floor. The one I was following rises and falls with the roll of the landscape. One minute you're walking through forested lowlands at the end of a lake, the next you're clambering up a rugged, rocky slope, heart pounding and legs complaining. The trail circumnavigates Little Slide Lake, spitting you back at your vehicle after eight vigorous miles of ridge walking and stunning lake views. The ups and downs are constant and the energy you expend is far greater than the limited distance would suggest. But back to that revelation.

I had been thinking about doing the hike all winter. It's a good stretch for the legs and lungs and a fine opportunity to spend some quality time alone. I've done it many times before and I have always enjoyed it. Yet I procrastinated. Why was I having such a hard time getting moving? It's not as if spending too much time watching television or endlessly going to the same web sites time after time is sufficiently stimulating to keep the mind engaged. I needed the exercise. I enjoy the walk. What was stopping me?

Part of my pathetic little brain said, 'It's annoying getting your stuff together and putting your boots on. It's going to be muddy, or slushy, or icy – you might slip and hurt yourself. You're going to be tired. Your muscles are going to ache for days. It'll be boring.'

So day after day I lingered, annoyed with myself for being so idle yet unable or unwilling to take those first steps.

It's the same with riding. In early spring I often look at the thermometer and the road conditions, think about getting ready for a ride and then say…nah! The bikes are ready. I've been dreaming of riding all winter, but when the conditions seem perfect and all the stars are aligned, I resist.

It's amazing how even little things can throw you off. On one of the first nice days this spring (2021), I packed a few things on to the Suzuki Cavalcade for an all-day ride up towards the Ottawa valley. A couple of days before I'd noticed that the self-cancelling indicators had stopped working. I assumed it was a fuse or something minor and carried on, not much concerned by this trivial inconvenience.

But as I set out to ride, the first thing I noticed was that the speedometer wasn't working. I switched on the cruise control – that was dead too. I could have carried on. Everything else was working fine. The bike was running smoothly, and I have a pretty good idea of what speed I'm travelling just by looking at the tachometer. For that matter, I have a GPS onboard which could have given me an accurate speed. Did I continue? No. I circled back home to investigate. It was such a little thing but it had thrown me enough of a curve that my enthusiasm for a long ride had evaporated. I knew I'd be fretting about that

malfunctioning speedometer all day.

The irony is, had this happened part-way through a multi-day trip, I would have shrugged it off and carried on, barely giving it a thought. Once again, those first few miles leaving home are always the hardest.

Since I have other bikes, I parked the Suzuki, and the next time I ventured out it was on my 1972 Moto Guzzi Eldorado. If you've watched any of my numerous Youtube videos, you can hardly have avoided noticing that neither the tach, nor the speedometer work on the Eldorado. The tach usually sits entirely still, showing 3000rpm, regardless of how the engine is spinning, while the speedometer flails around wildly, usually telling me I'm travelling at 120mph, when I'm not even going half that fast. Yet, I barely give it a second thought. I suppose I expect perfection from my 'new' (1986) Suzuki, while the older Eldorado gets a 'by' for any flaws and deficiencies because of its advance years. On reflection, I just used the ailing speedo as an excuse to head back to the house, park the bike and park my backside on the couch.

Incidentally, a few weeks later, I delved behind the bodywork, disconnected the Suzuki's speedometer cable and ordered a new one. When I connected it, it still didn't work. The speedometer drive-box was seized, so back to the computer with credit card handy to order a new one. Why don't I investigate these things fully at the time? I guess I'm just not that thorough.

The point of all this rambling is that it is so easy to let minor obstacles and irritations to get in the way of doing things that you love. Whether hiking or riding, once I've actually got myself moving and away from the house, I never regret it. I can't think of a single time I've been riding or hiking and wished I was back home.

You might think that with approaching geezerdom, I'd have become more mellow, more settled in my ways, and more eager to lie on the couch watching TV than straddling a truculent old motorbike and riding off into the distance. Nothing could be further from the truth.

As I see the years ahead of me shrinking, if anything, I'm keener than ever to saddle up and head for the horizon.

Do it while you still can – that's my mantra. The days when you can't will arrive soon enough.

Do it while you still can

ABOUT THE AUTHOR

Nick Adams emigrated to Canada from the UK in 1977 to work for the Ontario government as an archaeologist. He soon fell in love with Canada's north and, for the past few years, has been exploring it by canoe and motorcycle.

Over the years, as the number of bikes in his garage has increased, so have his travels in Canada as he seeks out distant places and deserted highways. Eschewing modern adventure bikes, Nick prefers to ride his older bikes, arguing that a few road-side breakdowns and 'tune-up's' are an integral part of any adventure.

From time to time, he returns to the UK to 'get a breath of Britain' by hiking some of its many long-distance footpaths and riding around visiting friends and relatives on rented motorbikes. Writing about his trips and sharing them with others doubles the pleasure. He is a regular contributor to 'RealClassic' magazine and frequently posts to on-line motorcycle forums.

OTHER BOOKS BY NICK ADAMS

FICTION

The Ghosts of Holleford Lake
(Book 1 in the 'Friends of the Dead' series)
Evil at Lac La Mort
(Book 2 in the 'Friends of the Dead' series)

NON FICTION (motorcycle travel)

Beyond the Coffee Shop
The Road to Missinabie
Beyond the Bypass
Eldorado to the Klondike
Riding in the Time of the Plague

NON FICTION (hiking/motorcycle travel in the UK)
Actually, I'm English

NON FICTION (autobio)
Archaeology: Life in the Trenches

All books are available on **Amazon** in paperback and digital format (Kindle), or as audiobooks narrated by the author through **Amazon** and **Audible**.

For more information, please refer to my web site at:

www.nickadamswriting.com

Printed in Great Britain
by Amazon